Part-time Baker

Part-time Baker

Simple bakes without the stress

Florence Stanton

Photography by Maja Smend

Carnival

Introduction

This world of faster, quicker, busy, always on, emails, buzzes, notifications, and a never-ending to-do list, can often leave us feeling like we have no time for our favourite things: the things that spark joy and make us feel at peace in ourselves. *Part-Time Baker* is a book for those who, like me, find baking to be a stress-reliever and a time to slow down, and also for people who are just beginning to explore baking as a new hobby. This is a book of recipes that don't require special skills, knowledge, ingredients or equipment. You can pick this up at the end of a busy day, put your finger on anything in the table of contents, and know that you are on your way to creating something delicious with minimal stress.

Part-Time Baker was born when I was working a 9-5 public relations job in Aberdeen, then baking at home to relax, to show love to my partner, and making things to take into work the next day (and who doesn't love the person who shows up on a dreary Tuesday with homemade cake). I didn't want to spend hours over laborious macarons or tiered cakes that likely wouldn't end up looking like they do in the photos. I wanted reliable bakes that were versatile enough to put a personal spin on without reinventing the wheel or being worried about the outcome. This, plus some strong encouragement from loved ones, was the birthplace of my social media and recipe website, Tasting Thyme. From there, while still working in PR, I found comfort in a community of so many people who, like me, wanted to create wonderful-tasting things without having hours to spend in grocery stores and in the kitchen. Through the Covid lockdowns of 2020-2021, when I no longer had a commute to work, I realised the amount of time I was spending in the kitchen baking pretty much equated to a part-time job, and I loved it!

I often baked with my mum when I was a child, but as I moved through my late teens and early twenties I stopped. I had developed a shaky relationship with food, over-exercising and under-fuelling; my hair fell out, my skin looked grey, and I was permanently exhausted. When I started baking again, I realised I could eat, without guilt – baking shifted my mindset surrounding food; it was my singular refuge. I would create my own bakes with no knowledge of how many calories were in a portion, or what 'one portion' even looked like. I think with so many supermarket products having numbers printed so clearly, it can creep into how we choose what we eat, opting for items that aren't what we actually want.

By removing this, I found I regained a love of food without numbers circling in my head. I learned to enjoy food for what it really is, a way to share and show love, moments of delight and memories that are so much more important than a basic number or something worthy of guilt. This is something I've spoken about on my social media, and I think is really important to keep sharing. I cannot ever overstate how powerful a tool baking can be in your arsenal against a busy world!

The chapters are laid out by time of day, from when you wake up to those late-night snacks before bed. Food plays a pivotal role in our daily lives, and the hope is that you can pick up this book at any moment and know there is something to suit how you're feeling, the time of day and the mood you're in – with stress alleviation, an act of self-care, and good food always being the outcome. There is something about sitting down with a plate of delicious food with someone you love (and remember, you can be that someone you love), that soothes the mind and soul.

Many of the recipes in this book are fabulous for all the family, and there are plenty of simple ideas for beginner bakers and for those looking for something that requires minimal engagement of the brain. We may not all have the same 24 hours in a day, and this book aims to fit in to anyone's schedule – carving out time for you to do something you love, which is so crucial to our wellbeing. Most of the bakes can be transported to work or school, made for dinner parties, date nights, a girls' night, or simply eaten while standing at the kitchen counter with a large spoon – the epitome of self-care and self-love.

The versatile nature of my recipes means you can change them to suit what you have in your fridge or cupboard, and what you can source at the supermarket! Some of the recipes not listed as vegan can be veganised (for recipes that don't feature eggs, such as bagels, focaccia, oatcakes, shortbread and crumbles, feel free to swap the dairy for dairy-free equivalents), and likewise, if it is vegan, you can easily add cheese or use regular butter/dairy products. It's so important that these recipes feel as approachable as possible, so everything from the bread recipes to pastries are ideal for beginners.

It has been such a joy compiling, testing and trying all these bakes – not just for me but for all my friends and family who have gotten so many samples as we nail down the final list! Everything here has been tested with the mindset of a beginner baker, ensuring that instructions are clear and easy to follow and with no recipe that requires a certain level of skill. It is a highlight of my day to see the creations people make with these recipes, so please do share them with friends but also online – tagging me in your bakes on social media. And a final note before you dig in, this is not intended as a coffee table book that looks nice but unused – nothing makes me happier than those family cookbooks with edits written in, molten butter spills, folded corners and pages that are almost falling apart and I'd love for this to become one of those books for you.

Now, let's make something delicious!

Ingredients, Baking with Yeast & Equipment

Ingredients

For most recipes, I use the same simple ingredients across multiple bakes to help keep costs down, maximise fridge space and avoid confusion.

DAIRY: Use full-fat dairy products whenever possible. Butter, milk, cream cheese, cream, and so on, provide texture and structure to bakes, and using low-fat versions of these may result in a less desirable outcome! Unless otherwise stated, use unsalted butter. Swapping butter for margarine is often fine, but avoid this when making pastry dough.

SALT: I add salt to most of my bakes, which brings out the flavour and gives greater control over the salt content than using salted butter.

EGGS: Based on UK sizing. If you are in the US, size them up x1 (e.g., a medium in the UK is a large in the US). Use free-range/pasture-raised eggs wherever possible. I recognise baking ingredients can quickly add up in terms of cost, but if it is within your means to buy eggs from free-range birds, you'll see a happier difference in yolk colour compared to those from caged birds.

BAKING POWDER/BAKING SODA: Supermarket own-brand products are absolutely fine for these, but check the use-by dates on raising agents. They tend to expire after 6 months, at which point they will no longer actively work to raise your bakes.

CHOCOLATE/COCOA POWDER: For cocoa powder in brownies and seriously chocolate-heavy bakes, the Dutch-processed stuff is great, but isn't 100 per cent necessary. The same goes for the chocolate you use. Some people much prefer using the nicer chocolate, but when it's all mixed in, supermarket own-brand is absolutely fine. It's up to you!

On this note, wherever chocolate is an 'add-in' (chocolate chips/chunks that go into a batter, for instance), do play around with the chocolate you like – whether it's milk/dark/white. I regularly get messages on social media along the lines of 'I loved your Kinder Bueno blondies, how can I make them with Snickers?'. For blondies, brownies, cookies and more, you can simply sub a like-for-like without needing to do anything else.

While the recipes in this book use a microwave to melt chocolate, you can use a double boiler instead. Bring a small saucepan of water to a simmer, and add the chocolate to a heatproof bowl that's large enough to sit on top of the pan. Place the bowl of chocolate on top of the saucepan. Keep stirring the chocolate and keep the heat low until it has melted. Ensure no water boils over into the chocolate.

YEAST & BREADMAKING: Check your yeast hasn't expired by mixing it with warm water and a little sugar. It should 'bloom' and look bubbly after letting it rest for about 5 minutes (I usually use this time to get my other ingredients out and weighed). If not, dump it and buy new yeast! Similarly, not all yeast varieties are the same: active dry yeast, instant dry yeast, fast-acting instant yeast, and bread-machine yeast all behave slightly differently. Across the book, I use fast-acting instant yeast.

Baking with yeast

When making a yeasted dough, the rise times may vary depending on the temperature, humidity and altitude of where you live. The bread recipes in this book were tested when we lived in a 100+ year-old building in the north of Scotland. The key is volume: you are always looking for the dough to double in size in the first rise. If you are in a particularly cold climate, make use of radiators, boiler cupboards, or even put the oven on to its very lowest setting to get the dough rising. If you live in a very warm climate, try to keep the dough cooler (but keeping it out of direct air conditioning).

Equipment

There is very little technical equipment or skill needed for the recipes in this book. My goal is that you can create the exact same thing as you see in the photos without any experience in the kitchen! Here is a list of things I recommend having in your kitchen:

ELECTRIC MIXER: Even a handheld, store own-brand one will do the job far better than relying on hand-mixing everything. If you have a stand mixer, you'll find life even easier, but it's not at all necessary!

TINS/PANS: The majority of bakes in the book are made using a 20cm (8in) square baking tin, large flat baking trays, a 900g (2lb) loaf tin, or a 23cm (9in) loose-bottomed cake tin. The dark metal ones are the best, but any metal trays will work! For things like the mini loaves, these tins are easy to source online.

UTENSILS: A balloon whisk, a spatula and a wooden spoon are crucial. Everything else is optional! (E.g. rolling pins can be a wine bottle, ice cream scoops can just be tablespoons...)

A QUICK NOTE ON OVEN TIMINGS: The timings I've used are based on my own oven, and everyone's oven can be a little different. If you know you have an oven that runs hot/cold, try using a lower shelf or shifting the times by a few minutes. If you're really unsure how your oven behaves, a cheap oven thermometer will help! No peeking in the oven mid-bake unless specified!

start your day

Chocolate & Hazelnut Pull-apart Loaf

SERVES: 8

1 x 7g/¼oz sachet fast-acting
instant yeast

1 tbsp granulated sugar

250ml (8fl oz/1 cup) tepid
water

55g (2oz) butter, melted, plus
a little extra for brushing the
finished loaf

200g (7oz/1½ cups) strong
white bread flour

150g (5½oz/generous 1 cup)
plain (all-purpose) flour, plus
extra for dusting

3 tsp fine sea salt

200g (7oz) chocolate hazelnut
spread

75g (3oz) hazelnuts, crushed

a little flavourless/mild-
flavoured oil, for greasing

Another chocolate for breakfast situation? Yes! This 'pull-apart' loaf, made of layers of pillowy bread dough sandwiched around chocolate hazelnut spread, is a real treat to eat while it's still warm.

Combine the yeast, sugar and tepid water in a large bowl, or the bowl of a stand mixer fitted with the dough hook attachment, stir and leave it to sit and let the yeast 'bloom' for 10 minutes (it should look bubbly).

Add the melted butter and both types of flour to the yeast mixture, along with the salt, and bring together. Once a shaggy dough has formed, knead for 10 minutes by hand on a floured surface, or 5–7 minutes in the mixer on medium speed, until it forms a smooth, springy ball. Lightly oil the bowl, place the dough back into it, cover with a clean tea towel and leave to rest in a warm place for 1 hour or until doubled in size.

Lightly oil a 900g (2lb) loaf tin (pan). Divide the dough into about 12 balls then roll each ball of dough flat on a floured surface and top it with chocolate hazelnut spread in an even layer. Top with some crushed hazelnuts, saving some to scatter over at the end. Fold each piece of chocolate-covered dough in half, creating a semi-circle. Place these pieces of dough in the tin with the folded edge at the bottom. Leave to prove in a warm place, covered with a tea towel, for 30 minutes.

Preheat the oven to 180°C fan (200°C/400°F/Gas 6).

Bake the risen loaf in the oven for 40 minutes until golden brown on top.

Remove from the oven, brush with some melted butter, sprinkle with the remaining crushed hazelnuts and serve warm!

The loaf will keep well for up to 2–3 days in an airtight container. Give it a 20-second flash in the microwave to reheat, if you like.

Banana & Walnut Streusel Muffins

MAKES: 9 MUFFINS

3 medium bananas

110g (3¾oz) butter, melted

75g (2½oz/⅓ cup) soft light brown sugar

50g (1¾oz/4 tbsp) granulated sugar

1 tsp vanilla extract

1 medium egg

200g (7oz/1½ cups) plain (all-purpose) flour

1 tsp baking powder

1 tsp bicarbonate of soda (baking soda)

pinch of fine sea salt

½ tsp ground cinnamon

50g (1¾oz) walnuts, finely chopped

Streusel topping

1 tbsp butter

2 tbsp plain (all-purpose) flour

3 tbsp rolled oats

2 tbsp soft light brown sugar

25g (1oz) walnuts, chopped

These banana muffins, topped with a little streusel mixture, are the easiest you'll ever make. Streusel is essentially the same as a crumble topping, made up of oats, flour, sugar and butter. The crumbly texture of the streusel meets the moist muffin to create a delightful bite! The riper the bananas the better here, even as far as fully brown, as these are sweeter and add a richer flavour.

Preheat the oven to 180°C fan (200°C/400°F/Gas 6) and line 9 holes of a 12-hole muffin tin (pan) with paper cases.

Peel the bananas and mash them in a large bowl, then add the melted butter, both sugars, vanilla and egg and stir until just combined. Combine the dry ingredients – the flour, baking powder, bicarbonate of soda (baking soda), salt, cinnamon and walnuts – in a bowl then add them to the wet ingredients and stir together very gently with a wooden spoon until only just combined.

Spoon the batter evenly among the paper cases, filling them two-thirds full.

In a small bowl, combine the streusel topping ingredients with a fork – the mixture should be pretty dry and crumbly. Sprinkle it evenly over the muffin batter, trying to cover the batter entirely for the best result, then bake in the oven for 20–25 minutes, until the tops are golden brown and when a skewer is inserted it comes out clean.

Remove from the oven, transfer to a wire rack and leave to cool.

The muffins will keep well for up to 2 days in an airtight container.

Why not try

Swirling a little caramel or chocolate sauce through the muffin batter in the cases before adding the topping and baking.

White Chocolate, Raspberry & Pistachio Pastry Braid

SERVES: 8

100g (3oz) white chocolate, broken into pieces

320g (11¼oz) all-butter puff pastry (a ready-rolled sheet is best)

100g (3½oz) raspberries

75g (3oz) pistachios, shelled and coarsely chopped

milk, for brushing

a little sugar, for sprinkling (optional)

a little icing (powdered) sugar, to serve

A store-bought pastry situation, packed full of white chocolate, raspberries and pistachios. This is a really pretty bake and I can promise everyone will be in awe: this is perfect for those social media shots! You can make it the night before and bake it in the morning if that's easier.

Preheat the oven to 200°C fan (220°C/430°F/Gas 7) and line a large rectangular baking tray with baking parchment (or a silicone liner).

Melt the white chocolate in a microwave in 20-second intervals, stirring regularly to make sure it doesn't burn. Leave to cool.

Unroll the pastry sheet on the lined tray then roll it out to the size of the tray. Spread the melted (but no longer hot) chocolate down the middle of the rectangle, lengthways, creating a long rectangle of chocolate and leaving pastry on either side. Sprinkle three-quarters of the raspberries and pistachios on top (saving some to decorate) then use a sharp knife to cut slits about 3cm (1¼in) apart into the pastry on each side, up to where the chocolate is. Take these 'strips' of pastry and fold them into the centre to make a braid-like shape. Nip the pastry at the ends to seal. Brush with milk and sprinkle over a little sugar (if using), then bake in the oven for 20 minutes. Reduce the oven temperature to 180°C fan (200°C/400°F/Gas 6) for a further 10 minutes until golden brown.

Remove from the oven and leave to cool. Sprinkle with the remaining raspberries, pistachios and icing (powdered) sugar to decorate.

Cheat's Almond Croissants

MAKES: 4 ALMOND CROISSANTS

4 store-bought plain croissants

Frangipane-style filling

120g (4¼oz/1 cup) ground almonds

70g (2½oz) butter, at room temperature

110g (3¾oz/½ cup) caster (superfine) sugar

1 large egg, beaten

½ tsp almond extract

To decorate

flaked (slivered) almonds, toasted

icing (powdered) sugar

Did you know that many almond croissants are made from leftover plain croissants and added almond paste?! Almond croissants are usually my go-to breakfast when I'm in a hurry and passing a café. This way, you can make them at home for a fraction of the cost with the same gorgeous results. They are definitely best served warm with a dusting of icing (powdered) sugar.

Preheat the oven to 180°C fan (200°C/400°F/Gas 6) and line a large baking tray with baking parchment (or a silicone liner).

Make the filling by combining the ground almonds, butter and sugar in a large bowl. Add the egg and almond extract and mix to form a paste.

Arrange the croissants on the lined tray. Cut a hole in the croissants along the side, to create an opening, then fill each croissant with a tablespoon of the almond paste. Spread the remaining paste on top.

Bake in the oven for 12–13 minutes, until crisp and golden.

Remove from the oven, sprinkle with some flaked (slivered) almonds, dust with icing (powdered) sugar, and serve!

Honey & Oat Loaf

PROVING TIME: 1 HR

BAKE TIME: 35-40 MINS

TOTAL TIME: 1 HR 50–55 MINS

SERVES: 12

mild cooking oil spray

325g (11½oz/2⅓ cups) strong white bread flour, plus extra for dusting

50g (1¾oz/generous ½ cup) rolled oats, plus an optional extra handful for sprinkling

1 x 7g/¼oz sachet fast-acting instant yeast

2 tsp fine sea salt

230ml (7¾fl oz/1 cup) tepid water

3 tbsp runny honey

1 medium egg, beaten, for brushing (optional)

Why not try

1. Warm butter and extra honey drizzled over

2. Thick-cut orange marmalade

3. Brie and bacon

There is truly no better smell than freshly baked bread. Just imagine that plus cosy honey and oat tones that will flood your kitchen with the most delicious scent – this Honey and Oat Loaf really has it all. Despite this being a gorgeous loaf for any occasion, it only requires a few ingredients and one prove then you simply bake until those smells are radiating and the crust is golden! An ideal vessel for all your favourite toast toppings or sandwich fillings (or do as I do and just smother it in butter).

Lightly grease a 900g (2lb) loaf tin with oil to prevent the loaf from sticking.

Put the flour, oats and yeast in a large bowl, and then add the salt, keeping it separate from the yeast. Make a well in the centre. Pour the water and honey into this well and combine. If using a stand mixer, use a dough hook attachment and mix on medium speed for 5 minutes until smooth. If doing it by hand, once combined, tip onto a lightly floured surface and knead for about 8 minutes or so.

Form the dough into an oval shape and put it in the greased tin. Cover with a clean tea towel and leave to rise for 1 hour until doubled in size.

Preheat the oven to 160°C fan (180°C/350°F/Gas 4).

If using, brush the beaten egg over the loaf (this gives it a golden colour) and sprinkle over a handful of extra oats if you like. Bake in the oven for 35–40 minutes until golden brown.

Remove from the oven and let the loaf cool in the tin, before turning it out, slicing and eating! The loaf will keep for a few days, stored in an airtight container, and can be sliced then frozen.

Triple Chocolate Chunk Muffins

MAKES: 6 MUFFINS

155g (5½oz/generous 1 cup) plain (all-purpose) flour

1 tsp baking powder

110g (3¾oz/½ cup) granulated sugar

1 tbsp cocoa powder

75ml (2½fl oz/⅓ cup) milk

1 medium egg

60g (2¼oz) butter, melted

2 tbsp vegetable oil

75g (2½oz) milk chocolate, coarsely chopped into chunks

75g (2½oz) white chocolate, coarsely chopped into chunks

The ultimate breakfast treat for me has got to be chocolate muffins. These involve cocoa powder, milk and dark chocolate for a dreamy (but oh so easy) chocolate bomb! Start to finish, they're ready in 35 minutes, meaning you can whip these up and have warm, melty muffins ready for any occasion!

Preheat the oven to 180°C fan (200°C/400°F/Gas 6) and line a 6-hole muffin tin (pan) with paper cases.

Combine all the dry ingredients – the flour, baking powder, sugar and cocoa powder – in a large bowl. Make a well in the dry mixture then add the milk, egg, melted butter and vegetable oil. Stir together very gently with a wooden spoon until only just combined.

Add the chocolate chunks and stir in briefly. Spoon the batter evenly among the paper cases and bake in the oven for 18–20 minutes, until the tops are a dark brown and a skewer inserted into a muffin comes out clean.

Remove from the oven, transfer to a wire rack and leave to cool before eating (although they are so great eaten warm!).

The muffins will keep well for up to 2 days in an airtight container.

10 mins   **HANDS-ON TIME**

COOK TIME: 20–25 MINS

TOTAL: 30–35 MINS

3-Ingredient Chocolate Twists

MAKES: 7 TWISTS

70g (2½oz) instant custard powder

150ml (5fl oz/⅔ cup) boiling water

320g (11¼oz) all-butter puff pastry

a little flour, for dusting

75g (2½oz) milk chocolate chips

1 medium egg, beaten, for brushing (optional)

Is there really anything better than pastry for breakfast? These are just like those chocolate torsades you find in coffee shops, except they're much cheaper and so much easier to make than you might expect. If you're looking to impress, you could definitely make the pastry yourself, but I like to keep things easy until after a few cups of coffee. You only need three main ingredients for these chocolate twists, but they look so impressive nobody will ever know they only took you 10 minutes to prep!

Preheat the oven to 200°C fan (220°C/430°F/Gas 7) and line two large baking trays with baking parchment (or silicone liners).

Make the custard using the powder and boiling water, following the custard powder packet instructions – it'll be thick. Let it chill in the fridge for 10 minutes.

Remove the pastry from its packaging. If it's ready rolled, unroll it onto a floured surface; if it's a block, roll it out on a floured surface to a thickness of about 2cm (¾in), about 30 x 15cm (12 x 6in). With the short width closest to you, spread the custard over the pastry – the custard should be thick yet spreadable. Sprinkle the chocolate chips over the custard evenly, then fold the pastry in half from bottom to top and cut it into seven strips. Take each strip and, holding one end in each hand, twist it three or four times. Place on the lined baking trays with space between them to allow for them to expand. If using, brush the egg wash over the top (this will give it a super-golden shine). Bake in the oven for 20–25 minutes, checking regularly to ensure they don't burn – they should be a deep golden brown.

Remove and leave to cool on a wire rack, though I can never stop myself eating one while they're still warm!

The Ultimate Chocolate Brownies

MAKES: 9 BROWNIES

100g (3½oz) dark chocolate, chopped

170g (5¾oz) butter, melted

100g (3½oz/½ cup) granulated sugar

100g (3½oz/½ cup) soft light brown sugar

2 medium eggs

1 tsp vanilla extract

85g (3oz/generous ½ cup) plain (all-purpose) flour

30g (1oz) cocoa powder

100g (3½oz) white chocolate, coarsely chopped

100g (3½oz) milk chocolate, coarsely chopped

AKA the only brownie recipe you will ever need. Fudgy, gooey, chocolate-y and so versatile, they are a huge hit to share with friends/family/co-workers etc. (while I cannot guarantee a promotion as a result, they're a guaranteed hit!). Base all future brownies on this, and simply change up what add-ins you use for top results every time.

Preheat the oven to 180°C fan (200°C/400°F/Gas 6) and line a 20cm (8in) square brownie/baking tin with baking parchment.

Melt the dark chocolate in a microwave in 20-second intervals, stirring regularly to make sure it doesn't burn.

In a large mixing bowl, with an electric handheld whisk, or in the bowl of a stand mixer fitted with the beater attachment, whisk together the melted butter and both sugars for 3–5 minutes until totally combined. Add the eggs, one at a time, mixing after each addition, then add the vanilla extract and mix again. Gradually add the melted chocolate and mix to combine. Add the flour and cocoa powder and fold them gently into the wet mixture with a rubber spatula or wooden spoon until just combined. Fold in the chopped chocolate.

Transfer the batter to the lined tin and bake in the oven for 25–30 minutes until the mixture has a shiny crust on top, and just a little hint of wobble in the middle.

Remove from the oven and leave the brownies in the tin on a wire rack until totally cooled, then remove and slice!

The brownies will keep well for up to 5 days in an airtight container, and can also be frozen.

Mini-Egg Hot Cross Buns

MAKES: 8 BUNS

425g (15oz/3¼ cups) strong white bread flour, plus extra for dusting

50g (1¾oz/4 tbsp) granulated sugar

1 x 7g/¼oz sachet fast-acting instant yeast

pinch of fine sea salt

250ml (8fl oz/1 cup) milk, warmed a little (tepid)

50g (1¾oz) butter, melted

1 medium egg

150g (5½oz) chocolate Mini Eggs, crushed (see note)

Crosses

50g (1¾oz/⅓ cup) plain (all-purpose) flour

1 tbsp granulated sugar

6 tbsp warm water

Glaze

2 tbsp boiling water

2 tbsp granulated sugar

An Easter brunch special, these hot cross buns are a spin-off of the classic and one of my all-time favourite breakfast treats! The dough gets mixed up with lots of crushed mini eggs for a super-fun bake.

Combine the flour, sugar and yeast in a large bowl, and then add the salt, keeping it separate from the yeast. Make a well in the mixture. Alternatively, place the dry ingredients in the bowl of a stand mixer fitted with the dough hook. Whisk the milk, butter and egg in a jug, then add to the dry ingredients and use a wooden spoon (or the dough hook) to pull all the ingredients together and form a dough. Turn out the dough onto a lightly floured surface and use your hands to knead it for about 10 minutes (you may need to add more flour to make it more manageable), until smooth and it springs back a little when you press your finger into it, or knead it with the stand mixer.

Place the dough into a lightly oiled bowl, cover with a clean tea towel and leave to rise in a warm place for at least 1 hour, until it has doubled in size.

Turn out the risen dough onto a lightly floured surface and knock it back. Sprinkle over the crushed Mini Eggs and knead a few more times until all combined. Use a knife to divide dough into 8 equal pieces. Roll the pieces into balls, place on a baking tray lined with baking parchment (or a silicone liner), slightly spaced apart, cover with a tea towel and leave somewhere warm for another 20 minutes.

Preheat the oven to 180°C fan (200°C/400°F/Gas 6).

Make the crosses by combining the flour, sugar and water in a small bowl. Pour this mixture into a piping bag (or a sandwich bag then cut the tip off) and pipe crosses onto the buns. By now, the buns should be puffed up and shiny, and most likely touching one another.

Bake the buns in the oven for 20 minutes, rotating the tray halfway through, until golden brown.

Remove from the oven. Make the sugar glaze by combining the boiling water and sugar in a bowl then brush it over the warm buns. Leave to cool on a wire rack before demolishing.

The buns will keep well for up to 3 days in an airtight container.

Note

Mini Eggs can be a little tricky to cut – I recommend leaving them in the bag (slightly opened) and bashing them with a rolling pin.

Savoury Baked Cheesy French Toast

SERVES: 6

butter, for greasing

300g (10½oz) bacon (optional)

6 large eggs, beaten

400ml (14fl oz/1⅔ cups) milk

4 tsp Dijon mustard

100g (3½oz) Cheddar, grated

100g (3½oz) Gruyère or similar, grated

pinch each of sea salt and freshly ground black pepper

1 loaf (about 400g/14oz) of crusty bread, preferably stale

Putting a savoury spin on our breakfast chapter, this baked French toast is made in one large pan, making it ideal for families or to gather friends around! Use stale bread, cover it in cheesy goodness and add any veg that needs using (tomatoes and peppers work really well). It's a great one to make ahead, as it needs to sit around in the mixture for a while before baking – half an hour absolute minimum – so it can be prepped and sit overnight.

Grease a 1–1.5-litre (34–50fl oz) baking dish with butter.

If you're using bacon, cut it into small pieces and fry it in a frying pan (skillet) over a medium heat until cooked and crisping up. Let cool.

Whisk the eggs, milk, mustard, half of both the cheeses, the salt and pepper and bacon (if using) together in a large bowl.

Cut the bread into 1cm (½in)-thick slices, dip them into the cheesy mixture then arrange them in the greased dish (try to keep the bread leaning up against other slices). Pour the remaining milk mixture over the top of the bread, cover with foil and leave to chill in the fridge for at least 30 minutes.

Preheat the oven to 200°C fan (220°C/430°F/Gas 7).

Sprinkle the remaining cheese over the soaked bread and bake in the oven (uncovered) for 20 minutes. Cover with foil and bake a further 10 minutes, then remove from the oven and serve.

Tip

Depending on the size of your bread slices, you could use something more like a loaf tin as opposed to a larger baking dish – you want the bread well stacked together for best results, like a bread-and-butter pudding, where the bottom of the bread is sticky and wet, and the top gets crisp.

25 mins **HANDS-ON TIME**

RISING TIME: 1 HR 30 MINS

BAKE TIME: 20–25 MINS

TOTAL: 2 HRS 15–20 MINS

Strawberry Jam Brioche Swirls

MAKES: 12 SWIRLS

1 x 7g/¼oz sachet fast-acting instant yeast

220ml (7¾fl oz/scant 1 cup) milk, warmed a little (tepid)

1 large egg

85g (3oz) butter, melted

50g (1¾oz/4 tbsp) granulated sugar

440g (15½oz/3½ cups) strong white bread flour, plus extra for dusting

mild cooking oil spray

Filling

130g (4½oz) good-quality strawberry jam

icing (powdered) sugar, to decorate (optional)

Tip

The brioche dough might feel quite 'wet' but trust the process. Once you've added all the flour, see how it feels. It should be sticky and damp, but just about manageable. If you think it is still just too wet, add up to 50g (1¾oz/⅓ cup) more flour.

This is a real nostalgia moment for me, with happy memories of my mum always heating up brioche and serving it with the fancy jam for breakfasts in bed. These are comforting and wonderful eaten warm, although the fruity flavours mean they would suit an al fresco summer breakfast in the garden, made complete with fresh coffee and orange juice. Plain (all-purpose) flour works just as well as bread flour, so use whatever you have to hand.

Combine the yeast and milk in a large bowl, or the bowl of a stand mixer fitted with the dough hook attachment. Leave to sit and let the yeast 'bloom' for 5 minutes (it should look bubbly).

Add the egg, melted butter and sugar and mix to combine, then add about three-quarters of the flour and bring everything together to form a rough dough using your hands or the dough hook attachment. Gradually add the remaining flour until a smooth dough forms, then knead for 8–10 minutes (on a floured surface if kneading by hand), until smooth. Grease a bowl with oil, add the dough, cover with a clean tea towel and leave the dough to rise in a warm place for 1 hour, or until doubled in size.

Once doubled in size, punch down the dough, tip it onto a lightly floured surface, then roll it out to a rectangle about 38 x 20cm (15 x 8in). Spread the jam over the dough, leaving space at the top then, starting with the long side, roll the dough away from you to form a tight log. Use a serrated knife to cut the log evenly into about 12 rolls. Place the rolls flat side down onto a large baking tray or in a 23 x 33cm (9 x 13in) baking dish lined with baking parchment, spaced apart to allow them to expand.

Leave somewhere warm to prove for a further 30 minutes, covered with a tea towel, and preheat the oven to 160°C fan (180°C/350°F/Gas 4).

Bake in the oven for 20–25 minutes, until golden brown.

Remove from the oven and leave to cool. Dust with icing (powdered) sugar (if using) and serve!

Speedy Sesame Bagels

MAKES: 4 BAGELS

165g (5¾oz/generous 1 cup) self-raising (self-rising) flour

165g (5¾oz) full-fat Greek yoghurt

milk, for brushing (optional)

2 tbsp sesame seeds

This is by no means an authentic bagel recipe – these need only three key ingredients and very little of your time. There is no proving and barely any kneading, meaning you can pull together something that pretty closely resembles a bagel without all that extra hassle! These are perfect toasted and topped with cream cheese although, as always, play around with any toppings you like!

Preheat the oven to 180°C fan (200°C/400°F/Gas 6) and line a baking tray with baking parchment (or a silicone liner).

Combine the flour and yoghurt in a bowl with a spoon then bring together with your hands to form a dough. The dough should be a little shaggy and sticky.

Divide the dough into 4 pieces and roll each piece into a 7.5–10cm (3–4in)-long log. Shape into a ring, pressing the ends together to form a bagel shape. Place on the lined baking tray and brush with milk (if using – it gives them a lovely sheen), then top with the sesame seeds and bake in the oven for 20–25 minutes until golden brown and toasty.

The bagels will keep well for up to 2 days in an airtight container, or can be frozen.

Why not try

Swapping the sesame seeds for poppy seeds.

Roasted Grapefruit with Homemade Coconut Granola

SERVES: 4

Granola

40g (1½oz/scant ½ cup) rolled oats

70g (2½oz/½ cup) flaked (slivered) almonds

70g (2½oz) dried dates

40g (1½oz) coconut flakes

2 tbsp coconut oil (or any non-flavoured oil)

4 tbsp maple syrup

1 tbsp honey

2 fresh pink grapefruits

1 tbsp maple syrup

yoghurt, to serve

A lighter breakfast option for those who tend not to eat much until later in the day but want to take a little time to make something delicious. The granola batch is large enough to last for several breakfasts/snacks – just box it up in an airtight container and sprinkle it over yoghurt and other breakfast items!

Preheat the oven to 180°C fan (200°C/400°F/Gas 6) and line two large baking trays with baking parchment (or silicone liners).

Make the granola by combining all the ingredients in a large bowl. It should form a sticky mixture. Spread this onto a prepared tray, keeping it together in clumps. Bake in the oven for 10–15 minutes, until golden, then remove and let it cool before breaking it into chunks.

Cut the grapefruits in half, then cut a little off each end so they stand up with the flesh facing upwards. Brush over the maple syrup and place in the oven on the second tray for 15 minutes (the fruit can roast at the same time as the granola mixture is baking).

Serve the roasted grapefruits warm with a little yoghurt and a generous sprinkle of the granola. The remaining granola will keep in an airtight container for up to 1 week.

Lemon Curd Breakfast Danishes

MAKES: 12 DANISHES

Rough puff pastry

1 x 7g/¼oz sachet fast-acting instant yeast

200ml (7fl oz/scant 1 cup) milk, warmed a little

380g (13½oz/generous 2¾ cups) plain (all-purpose) flour, plus extra for dusting

pinch of fine sea salt

175g (6oz) cold butter, cubed

50g (1¾oz/4 tbsp) granulated sugar

2 medium eggs

Filling

150g (5½oz) full-fat cream cheese

1 medium egg

50g (1¾oz/4 tbsp) granulated sugar

3 tbsp lemon curd, plus extra to serve

Glaze

2 tbsp apricot jam

Another recipe that will set you up for the best possible weekend. These are so versatile, so do consider substituting the lemon curd for any fruit jam! They are cutesy, bakery-style Danishes, made with a pretty easy pastry recipe. If you're in a pinch, store-bought puff is fine – it provides a slightly different, but equally delicious, result.

Combine the yeast and warm milk in a large bowl and leave to 'bloom' for 5 minutes. It should look bubbly.

Combine the flour, salt and butter in a large bowl and rub together with your fingertips until the mixture has a breadcrumb-like texture. Add the sugar and mix to combine (you could use a food processor for this if you prefer).

Pour the yeast and milk mixture into the bowl, add one of the eggs (keep the other for the egg wash) and mix to fully combine. Leave to rise for 1 hour in a warm place, covered with a clean tea towel, or if making ahead of time, place in the fridge overnight covered with cling film (plastic wrap).

Once ready to bake, tip the dough onto a floured surface and roll it into a long, thin rectangle about 23 x 30cm (9 x 12in), then fold the dough like a letter: fold the bottom up by a third, then fold the top over this. Rotate the dough 90 degrees and repeat three times.

Divide the dough into 12 pieces, then roll the pieces into balls. Flatten each ball so it's about 7.5cm (3in) wide and place the balls onto two baking trays lined with baking parchment (or silicone liners). Cover with a tea towel and leave to prove in a warm place for 30 minutes.

Meanwhile, make the filling mixture by combining the cream cheese, egg, sugar and lemon curd in a bowl.

Preheat the oven to 180°C fan (200°C/400°F/Gas 6). Press down into the middle of each round of dough to create a well for the filling – this should be pretty large, leaving just a little bit of an edge to act as the 'crust'. Divide the filling across the pastries, brush the edges with beaten egg and bake in the oven for 15–20 minutes, until golden.

To make the glaze, mix the apricot jam with about 2 tablespoons of water to loosen it then brush it over the warm pastries.

Top with extra lemon curd, leave to cool on wire racks, then serve!

Why not try

1. Using another jam or preserve in the filling – raspberry is great!

2. Make savoury Danishes: mix the cream cheese with salt, fresh herbs and some grated cheese and omit the apricot jam glaze at the end.

3. Use chocolate spread or/and Biscoff in place of the lemon curd.

Carrot Cake Muffins with Cream Cheese Filling

MAKES: 6 MUFFINS

160g (5½oz/generous 1 cup) plain (all-purpose) flour

1 tsp baking powder

1 tsp ground cinnamon

1 tsp ground ginger

110g (3¾oz/½ cup) granulated sugar

pinch of fine sea salt

50g (1¾oz) butter, melted

80ml (2¾fl oz/⅓ cup) milk

2 tbsp plus 1 tsp vegetable oil

2 tsp vanilla extract

1 medium egg

200g (7oz) grated carrot

Cream cheese filling

50g (1¾oz) cream cheese

1½ tbsp granulated sugar

2 tbsp milk

Tip

Muffins are not the same as large cupcakes. They require lots of moisture and the absolute minimum amount of mixing to retain the best texture. If you want to tweak the recipe at all, aim to keep the dry/liquid ratio as similar as possible.

Make ahead, adding lots of grated carrot and warming spices, bake then eat on the go! These are packed full of goodness, but best of all is the cream cheese filling and swirl on top. This makes these muffins a little 'special' something, compared to a basic muffin. Feel free to double up the recipe to make a larger batch. For the best muffins, all you want is a wooden spoon – overmixing is the enemy of good muffins!

Preheat the oven to 180°C fan (200°C/400°F/Gas 6) and line a 6-hole muffin tin (pan) with paper cases.

Combine all the dry ingredients – the flour, baking powder, spices, sugar and salt – in a large bowl. Make a well in the dry mixture then add the melted butter, milk, oil, vanilla and egg. Add the grated carrot and stir together very gently with a wooden spoon, until only just combined.

Make the cream cheese filling by combining all the ingredients in a bowl.

Now build the muffins: add 1 tablespoon of muffin batter to each muffin case, add 1–2 teaspoons of the cream cheese filling, then cover with remaining muffin batter. Add a little of the remaining cream cheese filling to the top of the muffins and swirl it with a knife or chopstick for pretty muffins!

Bake in the oven for 15–20 minutes, until golden and a skewer inserted into a muffin comes out clean.

Remove from the oven, transfer from the tin to a wire rack and leave to cool (although they are fabulous while still slightly warm).

The muffins will keep for up to 2 days in an airtight container.

Banana & Peanut Butter Baked Oatmeal

10 mins — HANDS-ON TIME

BAKE TIME: 30–35 MINS

TOTAL: 40–45 MINS

SERVES: 6

butter, for greasing

150g (5½oz/generous 1½ cups) rolled oats

100g (3½oz) peanut butter

3 ripe bananas

1 tsp baking powder

200ml (7fl oz/scant 1 cup) oat milk (or other vegan milk)

70ml (21/3fl oz/⅓ cup) maple syrup

100g (3½oz) milk chocolate chips (optional)

Quick and easy enough for a work morning, this can be made ahead in a batch to scoop as and when needed, or you can scale it down for single servings (you'll need to use a smaller baking dish and cook for a shorter time if so). The versatility of this bake is huge: sub your nut butter, add chocolate chips and other nuts and fruits for something that suits whatever you fancy! Once baked and cooled, you can portion up the oatmeal for a ready-to-go breakfast.

Preheat the oven to 180°C fan (200°C/400°F/Gas 6) and grease a 23cm (9in) square baking dish with butter.

Combine the oats, peanut butter, one of the bananas and the baking powder in a large bowl, add the milk and maple syrup and stir together. If using, add the chocolate chips. Pour into the baking dish and spread the mixture out evenly. Peel the remaining 2 bananas and slice them in half lengthways then press them into the oat mixture, cut side facing upwards.

Bake in the oven for 30–35 minutes, until the edges are just beginning to turn golden.

Remove from the oven and leave to cool before slicing and serving.

30 mins **HANDS-ON TIME**

RISING AND PROVING:
1HR 45 MINS–2 HRS 30 MINS

BAKE TIME: 18–22MINS

TOTAL TIME: 2 HRS 33
MINS–3 HRS 22 MINS

Classic English Teacakes

MAKES: 6 TEACAKES

100ml (3½fl oz/scant ½ cup)
milk

35g (1¼oz) butter

100ml (3½fl oz/scant ½ cup)
cold water

340g (12oz/2½ cups) strong
white bread flour, plus extra
for dusting

1 x 7g/¼oz sachet fast-acting
instant yeast

4 tbsp granulated sugar

1 tsp ground mixed spice

1 tsp ground cinnamon

pinch of fine sea salt

65g (2¼oz) raisins (or other
dried fruit)

1 egg, for brushing (optional)

A timeless, classic bake, English teacakes are made of a simple 'enriched' dough (dough made with added eggs or butter), augmented with lots of dried fruit to create a treat that makes for a fabulous breakfast, especially when toasted and smothered in butter.

Put the milk and butter in a small saucepan and heat gently until the butter melts, then turn off the heat and add the water to cool it down.

Put the flour, yeast, sugar and spices in a large bowl, or the bowl of a stand mixer fitted with a dough hook attachment, then add the salt, keeping it separate from the yeast. Make a well in the centre then pour in the milk/butter mixture and mix until the dough comes together: if you're using a stand mixer, knead it for about 5 minutes, if you're doing it by hand, bring the dough together in the bowl, then knead on a lightly floured surface for 6–8 minutes before lightly oiling the bowl you used and returning the dough to the bowl. Cover with a clean tea towel and leave to rise in a warm place for 1–1½ hours until doubled in size.

Line two large baking trays with baking parchment (or silicone liners). Place the dough on a lightly floured surface, punch it down and sprinkle over the dried fruit. Fold the dough over the fruit and knead until the fruit is evenly dispersed throughout. Cut the dough into 6 equal pieces, then take a piece and roll it into a smooth ball. Place on the lined tray and repeat with the remaining pieces, placing 3 teacake dough balls on each tray. Cover with a tea towel and leave to rise in a warm place for 45 minutes–1 hour.

Heat the oven to 180°C fan (200°C/400°F/Gas 6). If using, beat the egg and with a pastry brush paint it over: this gives them a shiny finish. Bake in the oven for 18–22 minutes, until they are golden brown and sound hollow if tapped on the bottom.

Remove from the oven and transfer to a wire rack. Serve while still warm (or reheat gently in the oven/toast them) with lots of salted butter.

The teacakes will keep for up to 3 days in an airtight container.

elevate
lunchtime

Goat's Cheese, Fig & Walnut Tart

SERVES: 6

320g (11¼oz) ready-rolled all-butter puff pastry

a little flour, for dusting

125g (4½oz) goat's cheese

100g (3½oz) crème fraîche

4 fresh figs

75g (2½oz) walnuts, coarsely chopped

sea salt and freshly ground black pepper

handful of fresh rocket (arugula), to serve

This is one of those recipes that may have you debating whether it totally fits into the savoury category, but it's a wonderful thing for those who love a cheese course after a meal or the cheese/fruit combination. There is added salt to keep it as a lunchtime treat, and this will sit amazingly as part of a lunch, perhaps alongside a Waldorf salad!

Preheat the oven to 180°C fan (200°C/400°F/Gas 6) and line a large baking tray with baking parchment (or a silicone liner).

Roll out the pastry on a floured surface to create a rectangle a little smaller than your baking tray – it should be about 1cm (½in) thick – and place it on the tray.

Mix together the goat's cheese and crème fraîche in a bowl and season with salt and pepper. Spread this mixture onto the pastry, leaving an edge of about 2.5cm (1in) around the border of the pastry to create crusts.

Thinly slice the figs lengthways and scatter them over the goat's cheese mixture, then add the chopped walnuts.

Bake in the oven for 30 minutes, until cooked through and the edges are a rich golden colour. Remove and leave to cool on a wire rack, scatter the rocket (arugula) over the top and serve!

RISING TIME: 1 HR

BAKE TIME: 20–25 MINS

TOTAL TIME: 1 HR 35–40 MINS

Cheat's Small-batch Ciabatta Rolls

MAKES: 4 ROLLS

1 x 7g/¼oz sachet fast-acting instant yeast

½ tsp honey

300ml (10fl oz/1⅓ cups) tepid water

260g (9½oz/1⅔ cups) strong white bread flour, plus extra for dusting

3 tsp salt

Sometimes you just want a quick, easy, one-proof, one-bowl bread recipe – this one will change your life. With minimal kneading and one-hour prove time, these still have that gorgeous fresh bread outcome without the hassle that normally comes with making ciabatta! Make them in the morning to have for lunch as sandwiches or with soup, or make to enjoy alongside a cosy dinner.

In a large bowl, or the bowl of a stand mixer fitted with the dough hook attachment, combine the yeast, honey and about 50ml (1¾fl oz/3½ tbsp) of the water. Leave to sit for 10 minutes to let the yeast 'bloom' (it should look bubbly).

Add the flour, salt and another 200ml (7fl oz/scant 1 cup) of the water and stir with a wooden spoon (or the dough hook attachment) until everything comes together. It should be sticky (sticky enough that it's hard to get off your hands!) and fairly difficult to handle. If not, add a little more of the water. Once all combined, sprinkle some flour over the top, cover the bowl with a clean tea towel and leave in a warm place for 1 hour until doubled in size.

Preheat the oven to 200°C fan (220°C/430°F/Gas 7) and sprinkle a baking tray with flour.

Remove the dough from the bowl, place it on the tray and cut it into 4 equal pieces. Roughly shape them into rectangles and sprinkle them with more flour. Just before baking, add a few ice cubes to a small baking dish and place in the bottom of the oven – this will create steam and give the bread a better crust.

Bake the rolls in the oven for 20–25 minutes until completely golden brown. If you tap the bottom of the rolls, they should sound hollow. Remove and leave to cool on a wire rack for at least 10 minutes before cutting into them. Serve with lots of salted butter.

The rolls will keep well for up to 5 days in an airtight container.

Tip

Your yeast doesn't need to be foaming up entirely; just some bubbles appearing on the surface tells us it's alive! Check your yeast's expiry date and always test it – if the package gives instructions to wait a little longer before it activates, allow for this.

RISING & PROVING TIME: 1 HR
30 MINS–2 HRS

BAKE TIME: 25 MINS

TOTAL: 2 HRS 15 MINS–2 HRS
45 MINS

Red Pesto & Mozzarella Bread Scrolls

MAKES: 12 SCROLLS

450g (1lb/3¾ cups) strong
white bread flour, plus extra
for dusting

1 x 7g/¼oz sachet fast-acting
instant yeast

1 tbsp granulated sugar

1 tbsp fine sea salt

3 tbsp olive oil

250ml (8fl oz/1 cup) tepid
water

mild cooking oil spray

Filling

190g (6¾oz) red pesto

200g (7oz) grated mozzarella

A one-bowl, minimal-kneading, minimal-fuss bread, packed with red pesto and shredded mozzarella for a really delightful thing. The smell of cheesy bread being baked is truly unmatched, and I highly recommend serving these alongside tapas-style snacks. This is another versatile recipe that you could play with – see below for ideas!

Put the flour, yeast and sugar in a large bowl, or the bowl of a stand mixer fitted with a dough hook attachment, then add the salt, keeping it separate from the yeast. Make a well in the mixture, add the olive oil and water and combine. Once it comes together, add up to 2 tablespoons more water if needed, until it comes together into a (slightly sticky) ball. Knead for 6–8 minutes with the stand mixer (or 8–10 minutes by hand, on a floured surface), then grease the bowl lightly with oil, place the dough in the bowl, cover with a clean tea towel and leave to rise in a warm place for 1 hour–1½ hours, until doubled in size.

Punch down the dough and transfer it to a lightly floured surface, then roll it out to a rectangle about 40 x 30cm (16 x 12in). Spread the pesto all over the dough, sprinkle over the cheese and press down on the cheese to 'compact' it a little. Starting on a long side of the rectangle, roll the dough up tightly into a large roll. Use either a serrated knife or dental floss (be sure not to use a flavoured one!) to cut the log evenly into about 12 rounds. Place onto a large baking tray lined with baking parchment (or silicone liner) or in a 23 x 33cm (9 x 13in) baking dish (greased with a little oil) cut side down and leave to prove in a warm place, covered with a tea towel, for 30 minutes.

Preheat the oven to 180°C fan (200°C/400°F/Gas 6).

Bake the scrolls in the oven for 25 minutes, until the dough is cooked through and the cheese is beginning to look a little crisp. They are best served warm, but are still wonderful once cooled! The scrolls will keep well for up to 4 days in an airtight container.

Why not try

1. Red onion chutney and grated Cheddar

2. Cranberry sauce and Brie (very festive)

3. Olive tapenade

Spring Green, Pesto & Courgette Flower Tart

SERVES: 6

1 medium leek, trimmed, washed and sliced into rings

1 tbsp salted butter

2 garlic cloves, minced

1 tbsp extra-virgin olive oil

75g (2½oz) asparagus spears, trimmed

2 large courgettes (zucchini) (including their flowers), thinly sliced

320g (11¼oz) ready-rolled all-butter puff pastry

a little flour, for dusting

200g (7oz) cream cheese

100g (3½oz) green pesto

sea salt and freshly ground black pepper

Perfect for a warmer day, this tart can be made using whatever fresh veg might be in season. Courgette (zucchini) flowers are increasingly easy to find in supermarkets, but this is not a necessity for the bake – just something to add a little wow factor! The vegetable weights are approximations, if you go over or under that's absolutely fine; the goal is simply to cover the tart.

Preheat the oven to 180°C fan (200°C/400°F/Gas 6) and line a large baking tray with baking parchment (or a silicone liner).

Place a large frying pan (skillet) over a medium-low heat, add the leek, butter and garlic and cook for 5–10 minutes until softened but not browned. Set the leek aside in a bowl, then in the same pan add the oil and fry the asparagus and courgettes (zucchini) for 5–10 minutes until softened and starting to blacken a little.

Roll out the pastry on a floured surface to create a rectangle a little smaller than your baking tray – it should be about 1cm (½in) thick – and place it on the tray. Spread on the cream cheese, leaving an edge of about 2.5cm (1in) around the border of the pastry to create crusts, then layer the cooked vegetables and the courgette flowers on top. Bake in the oven for about 20 minutes until the pastry is golden, then drizzle over the pesto, season with salt and pepper and serve!

Why not try

1. Beetroot and feta: roasted beetroot (beet) is a fantastic choice in place of greens.

2. Root vegetables like parsnips and carrots: pre-cook them before adding to the tart.

3. Assorted mushrooms – a selection of different mushrooms works really well.

Lentil Dal-inspired 'Sausage' Rolls

MAKES: 10 ROLLS

milk, for brushing (optional)

cumin seeds, to garnish (optional)

Rough puff pastry

125g (4½oz/1 cup) plain (all-purpose) flour, plus extra for dusting

125g (4½oz) cold salted butter, cubed

65ml (2¼fl oz/4½ tbsp) cold water

Filling

2 large red (bell) peppers, deseeded and cut into large chunks

olive oil, for drizzling

100g (3½oz) red lentils, rinsed and drained

55g (2oz) white bread (or store-bought breadcrumbs)

3 garlic cloves, peeled

2 tsp ras el hanout

2 tsp dried chilli flakes

2 tsp ground cumin

2 tsp dried oregano

sea salt and freshly ground black pepper

These little parcels of puff pastry filled with roasted red peppers, red lentils, breadcrumbs and a whole heap of spices make a mean meat-free sausage-roll alternative that will have even the most committed carnivores wanting more! Let me introduce you to my favourite homemade pastry: rough puff! It only takes a few minutes to pull together with a quick fold, but it means you get to humble brag about how you made a flaky pastry from scratch. Alternatively, feel free to use a 320g (11¼oz) packet of store-bought all-butter puff pastry. These 'sausage' rolls are photographed left on page 54–55.

If you are making your own pastry, combine the flour and butter by rubbing them together with your fingertips in a large bowl until roughly combined. You do not want to take it as far as breadcrumb-texture – there should still be bits of butter visible in places. Add the cold water and form into a ball, then wrap in cling film (plastic wrap) and chill for 30 minutes.

Remove the pastry from the fridge, unwrap it, then roll in one direction on a floured surface to form a long rectangle. Fold the top edge down to just below the middle, then fold the bottom edge over this, to form a square with three layers (this is called book end). Rotate this block 90 degrees and repeat. Wrap again and chill for another 20 minutes.

Meanwhile, make the filling. Preheat the oven to 200°C fan (220°C/430°F/Gas 7).

Put the pepper chunks on a baking tray, drizzle with a little olive oil, season with salt and pepper and roast for 20–30 minutes, until just browning at the edges. Remove, leaving the oven on and ready for the formed rolls.

Put the lentils in a large saucepan, add boiling water and cook for about 15 minutes over a high heat until soft. Drain.

Blitz the bread in a food processor until it forms fairly fine breadcrumbs, then transfer to a large bowl. (Or use ready-made breadcrumbs.)

Place the roasted red peppers and garlic cloves in the food processor and blitz until combined, then add to the large bowl, along with the drained lentils. Add all the seasoning and mix to combine. The texture should be like a thick, chunky paste (you don't want it too smooth – it needs to have some bite!).

Line two baking sheets with baking parchment (or silicone liners). Take the pastry out of the fridge, unwrap it and roll it out to a large, long rectangle, about 46 x 10cm (18 × 4in). Spread the filling across the long edge closest to you, keeping the filling mix in a cylinder/log shape and pressing it to keep tight. Leave about 2.5cm (1in) of the pastry uncovered on the side closest to you, and more room on the other side. Take the long edge of the pastry furthest away from you and roll it over the filling, keeping it as tight as possible, until you reach the end and have a log of pastry with the filling all inside, leaving a small 'overhang' – i.e., don't roll all the pastry to the very end. Crimp the overhang with the 'log' dough using a fork for neater rolls. Cut the pastry log into about 10 evenly sized sections and place on the lined baking sheets at least 5cm (2in) apart. Brush the tops of the rolls with a little milk and sprinkle with some cumin seeds, if you like, and bake in the oven for 15–20 minutes, until golden brown.

Remove from the oven and leave to cool on a wire rack (although they are fabulous eaten when warm). Let cool before boxing up.

The baked rolls will keep well in the fridge in an airtight container for up to 2 days, or can be frozen.

Tip
When rolling, keep the pastry tight to the filling as much as possible, otherwise the filling can leak out during baking. The pastry should stay cold, so try not to handle it too much.

HANDS-ON TIME

CHILL TIME: 20 MINS

BAKE TIME: 25 MINS

TOTAL: 1 HR 20 MINS

Mini Rainbow Tomato & Balsamic Galettes

MAKES: 4 GALETTES

Shortcrust pastry (makes about 320g/11¼oz)

100g (3½oz) cold salted butter, cubed

220g (7¾oz/generous 1½ cups) plain (all-purpose) flour, plus extra for dusting

2–4 tbsp cold water

Filling

400g (14oz) tomatoes, thinly sliced

2 tbsp balsamic vinegar

2 tsp dried oregano or similar Italian dried herb blend

8 tbsp full-fat cream cheese

1 medium egg, beaten, for brushing (optional)

sea salt and freshly ground black pepper

fresh basil, to garnish

Roasted is by far my favourite way to eat tomatoes. These galettes look so impressive but really take no time at all. Feel free to use store-bought shortcrust pastry, although the recipe is easy for any level of baking skill! The galettes are best served hot, alongside a big salad for a light summer dinner, or with some sides for a real feast!

If you are making your own pastry, combine the butter and flour by rubbing them together with your fingertips until the mixture resembles breadcrumbs (you could use a food processor for this). Add 2 tablespoons of the cold water and combine again. If the mixture is still dry and not coming together, add the rest of the cold water and bring together until a dough forms. Form into a ball, cover or wrap in cling film (plastic wrap) and chill for 20 minutes while the oven gets hot.

Preheat the oven to 200°C fan (220°C/430°F/Gas 7) and line two large baking trays with baking parchment (or silicone liners).

Place the sliced tomatoes in a bowl with the balsamic vinegar and dried oregano and season with salt and pepper. Mix and set aside.

Divide the dough into 4 pieces and roll each piece out to a thickness of 5mm (¼in) on a floured surface. Sprinkle flour on the lined baking trays and place the galette bases on the trays. Spread 2 tablespoons of cream cheese onto each galette base and create a circle, leaving a 2.5cm (1in) border around the edge. Top with the balsamic tomatoes, trying not to add too much of the liquid. Pull the galette pastry towards the centre bit by bit, leaving a good amount of the tomatoes exposed – don't worry about it looking neat! If using, brush the edges of the pastry with beaten egg (this will just give them an extra-golden shine).

Bake the galettes for about 25 minutes, until golden.

Remove from the oven and let cool slightly before serving. Top with fresh basil and serve.

Tip

To make vegan galettes, simply substitute the butter for vegan butter, and the cream cheese for the vegan alternative.

Red Onion & Mustard Sausage Rolls

MAKES: 12 ROLLS

1 tbsp olive oil

2 red onions, thinly sliced

6 good-quality pork sausages

2 tsp wholegrain mustard

1 tbsp honey

320g (11¼oz) all-butter puff pastry (or use the recipe for rough puff from the Lentil Dal-inspired Sausage Rolls recipe on pages 52-3)

sea salt and freshly ground black pepper

1 medium egg, beaten, for brushing

Cosy pockets of deliciousness and a British staple, these sausage rolls are a real crowd-pleaser. The combination of slightly caramelised onions, honey and mustard is one that is sure to have people coming back for more... My main piece of advice: double up if feeding a crowd – they're popular! These sausage rolls are photographed right on page 54–55.

Preheat the oven to 180°C fan (200°C/400°F/Gas 6) and line two large baking sheets with baking parchment (or silicone liners).

Heat the oil in a frying pan (skillet) over a low heat, add the red onions and cook for 15 minutes until softened and lightly browned.

Split the sausage skins and put the sausage meat into a large bowl. Add the mustard, honey and cooked onions, season with salt and pepper and mix to combine.

Roll the pastry into a large, long rectangle, about 46 x 10cm (18 x 4in). Spread the sausage filling across the long edge closest to you, keeping the filling mix in a cylinder/log shape and pressing it to keep tight. Leave about 2.5cm (1in) of the pastry uncovered on the side closest to you, and more room on the other side. Take the long edge of the pastry furthest away from you and roll it over the filling, keeping it as tight as possible, until you reach the end and have a log of pastry with the filling all inside, leaving a small 'overhang' – i.e., don't roll all the pastry to the very end. Crimp the overhang with the 'log' dough using a fork for neater sausage rolls. Cut the pastry log into about 12 evenly sized sections and place on the baking sheets at least 5cm (2in) apart. Brush the egg over the pastry, score some small diagonal lines in each roll to allow air to escape, then bake in the oven for 15 minutes, until the tops are golden brown. If any filling spills out, wait a few minutes once out of the oven before using the back of a spoon to push the filling back into the pastry. Serve warm or let cool before boxing up.

The baked rolls will keep well in the fridge in an airtight container for up to 2 days, or can be frozen.

Tip

These can be easily made vegetarian by using veggie sausage meat.

HANDS-ON TIME:

BAKE TIME: 20 MINS

TOTAL: 30 MINS

Smoked Salmon Filo Cups

MAKES: 10 FILO CUPS

250g (9oz) filo pastry

75g (2½oz) salted butter, melted, plus extra for greasing

75g (2½oz) crème fraîche

2 medium eggs, beaten

100g (3½oz) smoked salmon, coarsely chopped

handful of dill, chopped

handful of watercress, to serve

Another ridiculously easy party appetiser, these little cups will fly off the table. I use store-bought filo, then cut it into squares and layer it into a muffin tin. The filling gets scooped in then everything gets baked together for a really exciting snack! If you want to impress people (maybe the boss is coming and you're ready for that pay rise...), top them with caviar after baking.

Preheat the oven to 160°C fan (180°C/350°F/Gas 4) and grease 10 holes of a 12-hole muffin tin (pan) with a little butter.

Cut the filo pastry sheets into about 10cm (4cm) squares. Brush with melted butter and layer up 3 sheets, with the points at different angles to each other so they look a little messy! Place into the muffin tin and bake in the oven for 5 minutes, to par-cook them.

Mix together the crème fraîche, eggs, salmon and dill in a bowl then pour into the cups. Return to the oven to bake for 15 minutes, until cooked and the pastry is golden.

Remove from the oven, top with some watercress and serve either warm or cold.

Olive & Rosemary Focaccia Buns

MAKES: 12 BUNS

525g (18½oz/generous 4 cups) strong white bread flour, plus extra for dusting

1 x 7g/¼oz sachet fast-acting instant yeast

3 tsp fine sea salt

2 tsp garlic granules (or 1 garlic clove, minced)

6 tbsp extra-virgin olive oil, plus extra for greasing

350ml (12fl oz/1½ cups) tepid water

mild cooking oil spray

120g (4¼oz) olives, drained and chopped (I like to use Kalamata or green olives)

leaves stripped from some fresh rosemary sprigs, chopped

fresh basil leaves (optional)

Focaccia looks so impressive but actually isn't too complex to make. It is super versatile so feel free to play with other toppings, such as basil and Parmesan, sun-dried tomato, or jalapeño and Cheddar! Making them as buns is fun and gives a great crust to sponge ratio, perfect for scooping up the remnants of a good pasta sauce or soup. I highly recommend fresh rosemary, but dried is fine if you can't find any. Likewise, it's worth using good quality extra-virgin olive oil.

Put the flour and yeast in a large bowl, or the bowl of a stand mixer fitted with the dough hook attachment, and combine. Add the salt and garlic (making sure the salt isn't touching the yeast), then make a well in the dry mixture and pour in 3 tablespoons of the olive oil and all the warm water. Combine to form a dough – it should come together but be pretty sticky. If it doesn't come together, add a little more water. Knead for about 8 minutes, until soft and smooth (it will still be a little sticky) – if you are kneading it by hand, do this on a lightly floured work surface for a bit longer than if using a machine.

Liberally grease the bowl you used for the dough with oil, place the dough back in it, cover with a clean tea towel and leave to rise in a warm place for 30 minutes.

Now fold the dough: scoop the dough from one side of the bowl, pulling from the bottom and bringing it over to the other side. Rotate the bowl 90 degrees and repeat until you've completed 4 'folds'. Leave to rest for 30 minutes then repeat.

Liberally grease 12 muffin tin (pan) holes with oil. Add the chopped olives and most of the rosemary to the dough and knead to combine. Split the dough into 12 even-sized balls and place one ball in each greased muffin hole. Leave to prove in a warm place for 30 minutes.

Preheat the oven to 200°C fan (220°C/430°F/Gas 7).

Press dimples into the dough balls using your fingertips. Combine the remaining 3 tablespoons of olive oil with 2 tablespoons of water and brush this over the bread. Sprinkle over a little more chopped rosemary. Bake in the oven for 15–20 minutes until golden.

The buns will keep for up to 3–4 days in an airtight container.

Butternut Squash & Cheddar Scones

MAKES: 6–8 SCONES

200g (7oz) frozen butternut squash (or pumpkin)

350g (12oz/2¾ cups) plain (all-purpose) flour, plus extra for dusting

2 tsp baking powder

½ tsp bicarbonate of soda (baking soda)

1 tsp fine sea salt

50g (1¾oz) cold salted butter, cubed

100g (3½oz) mature Cheddar or similar hard cheese, grated

3 tsp dried rosemary

70ml (2⅓fl oz/⅓ cup) double (heavy) cream

1 medium egg, beaten, for brushing (optional)

fresh rosemary, to garnish (optional)

Tip

The key to really good scones is to keep everything as cold as possible until the moment they go in the oven.

I love a good, flaky scone and I truly love any bake involving cheese. The butternut squash in these autumnal savoury scones is subtle and sweet, and pairs so well with the herbs and spices. I love using frozen butternut squash in this recipe (or swapping it for pumpkin). Of course, fresh is fine too – just make sure it's totally cooked before using. These work perfectly with a good soup or stew.

First, cook the butternut squash. If using frozen, boil it for about 10 minutes, until totally soft, then drain and mash to make a puree. (If using fresh veg, roast them until totally cooked, remove the skin, then mash).

Preheat the oven to 200°C fan (220°C/430°F/Gas 7) and line a baking sheet with baking parchment (or a silicone liner).

Put the flour, baking powder, bicarbonate of soda (baking soda), salt and mashed butternut squash in a large bowl and quickly mix together, then add the butter and rub together with your fingertips until the mixture is evenly dispersed with pea-sized pieces of butter. Add the cheese, rosemary and cream and use a knife to bring everything together.

Tip the dough onto a floured surface and bring it together into a rough rectangle, then cut it into 3 pieces. Stack the pieces on top of one another and roll the dough out a little, then repeat the stacking. Roll the dough out to a thickness of 2.5–4cm and cut out 6–8 rounds using a 6cm (2½in) fluted cookie cutter – you should get about 8 if using a smaller cutter. Place the rounds on a plate or small tray and freeze for 10 minutes.

Brush the beaten egg over the scones (if using) – this gives the scones that super golden shiny finish! Add a little piece of fresh rosemary, if you like, and place on the lined baking sheet. Bake in the oven for 12–15 minutes, until golden.

Remove from the oven and transfer to a wire rack to cool.

The scones will keep well for up to 5 days in an airtight container.

Pepperoni Pizza Twists

SERVES: 4

Rough puff pastry (makes about 320g/11¼ oz)

125g (4½oz) cold salted butter, cubed

125g (4½oz/1 cup) plain (all-purpose) flour

65ml (2fl oz/¼ cup) cold water

Filling

150g (5½oz) pizza sauce (or marinara pasta sauce)

150g (5½oz) shredded mozzarella

100g (3½oz) Cheddar, grated

handful of fresh basil leaves

12 thin slices pepperoni

1 medium egg, beaten, for brushing (optional)

To create these little savoury flavour-bomb parcels, we make a rough puff pastry and spread it with marinara sauce, toppings and lots of cheese for pure deliciousness. They're great for quick lunches for the whole family (use store-bought all-butter puff pastry for a shortcut if you want something extra speedy). I'm a big advocate for playing around with toppings for these – caramelised onion chutney and goat's cheese, pesto, anything that needs using up really! This recipe can very easily be scaled up to make a larger batch.

If you are making your own pastry, combine the butter and flour by rubbing them together with your fingertips in a bowl until roughly combined. You do not want to take it as far as breadcrumb-texture – there should still be bits of butter visible in places. Add most of the cold water and form into a ball (adding the rest of the water if needed). Wrap in cling film (plastic wrap) and chill for 30 minutes.

Remove the pastry from the fridge, unwrap it, then roll it in one direction on a floured surface to form a long rectangle about 23 x 30cm (9 x 12in). Fold the top edge down to just below the middle, then fold the bottom edge over this, to form a square with three layers (this is called book end). Rotate the block 90 degrees and repeat. Wrap again and chill for another 10 minutes.

Preheat the oven to 220°C fan (240°C/460°F/Gas 8) and line two large baking trays with baking parchment (or silicone liners).

Take the pastry out of the fridge, unwrap it and roll it out to a thickness of about 1cm (½in), then cut it into 4 equal squares. Place two squares on each lined tray and, arranging the filling in a line diagonally across the middle, from the top left corner to the bottom right of each square, add the sauce, cheeses, basil, pepperoni and any other toppings. Wrap the pastry by folding the two corners opposite the line of filling (so that the filling is exposed) into the middle and pressing them together. If using, brush a little beaten egg over the pastry (this gives them an extra-golden shine). Bake in the oven for 12–15 minutes until golden brown.

Remove from the oven and leave to cool on a wire rack (although eating them warm is a real joy).

Tip

The key to good rough puff pastry is maintaining the streaks of butter and keeping it cold. If it loses its chill too much, i.e., during filling, place it back in the fridge for 10 minutes to get cold again before baking.

Leek & Potato Turnovers

MAKES: 4 TURNOVERS

250g (9oz) white potatoes (a waxy variety works best), peeled and cut into 5cm (2in) chunks

1 tbsp salted butter

2 medium leeks, trimmed, washed and thinly sliced

2 tsp dried rosemary, plus a little extra for sprinkling

splash of white wine (optional)

100g (3½oz) mature Cheddar, grated

5 tbsp cream cheese

320g (11¼oz) all-butter puff pastry (or use the recipe for rough puff from the Lentil Dal-inspired Sausage Roll recipe on page 52)

a little flour, for dusting

sea salt and freshly ground black pepper

1 medium egg, beaten, for brushing

Why not try

Bombay-style potatoes or leftover curry for the filling mixture. It sounds wild but trust me, this is a fabulous way to re-purpose something saucy and delicious!

We are huge leek lovers in our home, and the classic pairing with potato is a real delight. The filling comprises of these ingredients, plus rosemary, an optional splash of white wine, and cream cheese, which makes it beautifully rich and creamy. Pair that filling with buttery, flaky puff pastry and you're onto a winner. You can serve these up as they are, or alongside a cheeseboard/party sharing board and you can either make the puff pastry yourself (page 52), or use store-bought.

Cook the potatoes in a pan of boiling salted water until tender, then drain.

Melt the butter in a large frying pan (skillet) over a low-medium heat, add the leeks and fry for 10 minutes until softened but not browned, then add the cooked potatoes, dried rosemary and some salt and pepper. Increase the heat to medium and add the splash of wine (if using), then add the Cheddar and cream cheese. Stir until combined into a cheesy, creamy mixture. Set aside to cool.

Preheat the oven to 200°C fan (220°C/430°F/Gas 7) and line two or three large baking trays with baking parchment (or silicone liners).

Roll the pastry into a large 23 x 38cm (9 x 15in) rectangle on a floured surface and cut out four large squares of pastry (they don't need to be perfectly even). Divide the filling among the four pastry squares, placing over half of each square (as we'll be folding to create triangular pockets). Beat the egg and brush a little over the edges of the pastry squares, then seal the pockets by bringing the edges together to create triangles. Crimp with a fork to lock in the filling. Place the turnovers on the baking trays, at least 5cm (2in) apart, brush with a little more of the egg and scatter over some extra dried rosemary. Bake in the oven for about 20 minutes, until golden brown.

Remove from the oven and leave to cool a little on a wire rack. The turnovers will keep well in the fridge in an airtight container for up to 2 days.

Spinach & Feta Muffins

MAKES: 6 MUFFINS

190g (6¾oz/1⅓ cups) plain (all-purpose) flour

1 tsp baking powder

1 medium egg, beaten

80ml (2¾fl oz/⅓ cup) milk

50g (1¾oz) salted butter, melted

40ml (1¼fl oz/2½ tablespoons) vegetable oil

100g (3½oz) feta, crumbled

handful of fresh parsley, coarsely chopped

100g (3½oz) baby spinach, chopped

50g (1¾oz) pine nuts

For something that's great to make ahead for grab-and-go snacks through the week, these savoury muffins are absolutely perfect. They are great for breakfasts if you prefer a savoury start to the day, but also sit well at lunchtime in place of a boring sandwich, alongside some other snacks, of course. This recipe is easy to double up as needed, to make a bigger batch!

Preheat the oven to 180°C fan (200°C/400°F/Gas 6) and line a 6-hole muffin tin (pan) with paper muffin cases.

Combine the flour and baking powder in a large bowl using a wooden spoon, then make a well in the dry mixture, add the egg, milk, melted butter and oil and stir to combine. Add the crumbled feta, parsley and spinach and stir again. Divide evenly among the paper cases, top with the pine nuts and bake in the oven for 20 minutes, until golden.

Remove from the oven, transfer the muffins from the tin to a wire rack and leave to cool.

The muffins will keep well for up to 2 days in an airtight container in the fridge.

HANDS-ON TIME

BAKE TIME: 30–35 MINS

TOTAL: 50–55 MINS

Mini Quiches 3 Ways

MAKES: ABOUT 21 MINI QUICHES

320g (11¼oz) store-bought shortcrust pastry (or see page 56 if you want to make your own)

a little flour, for dusting

mild cooking oil spray

2 large eggs

150ml (5fl oz/⅔ cup) double (heavy) cream

150g (5½oz) mature Cheddar or similar hard cheese (Gruyère is great), grated

sea salt and freshly ground black pepper

Filling 1:

120g (4¼oz) smoked haddock

75ml (2½fl oz/⅓ cup) milk

3 tbsp finely chopped fresh chives

Filling 2:

3 tbsp coarsely chopped Parma ham

3 tbsp coarsely chopped sun-dried tomatoes

Filling 3:

1 red (bell) pepper, deseeded and diced

baby spinach, chopped

Quiche to me screams summer picnics, glasses of spritz, punnets of strawberries and so many other happy things. Following a basic recipe for these eggy/cheesy bites, you can run wild to your heart's content to incorporate any other ingredients that need using, or that are in season. Here, we've got a play on the Arnold Bennett omelette using smoked haddock, a ham and sun-dried tomato variation and a veggie option so the whole crowd should have something they like!

Preheat the oven to 180°C fan (200°C/400°F/Gas 6).

Roll out the pastry on a floured surface as thinly as possible without tearing it – about 5mm (¼in) thick. Lightly grease two 12-hole muffin or cupcake tins (pans) with oil and choose a cookie cutter that's slightly wider than the holes in the tins.

Punch out about 21 rounds of pastry and place them into the tin holes. Line each quiche tart shell with a piece of baking paper or cupcake case and fill with raw rice or baking beans. Bake in the oven for 10 minutes, then remove (carefully removing the paper and rice/beans too) and leave to cool.

Meanwhile, cook the haddock by putting it in a pan with the milk and simmering over a low heat for about 5 minutes, then drain the milk and pat the cooked haddock dry with kitchen paper.

Make the filling by whisking together the eggs, cream, Cheddar and some salt and pepper in a bowl. Fill the par-baked tartlets about two-thirds full with the egg mixture, then add the filling variations. Put chopped Parma ham and sun-dried tomatoes in a third of the tarts; flake the fish and add this and some chives to another third (save some chives to serve); and finally, the spinach and red pepper to the final third.

Bake in the oven for 20–25 minutes, until golden. Leave to cool on a wire rack before serving.

Thyme Oatcakes

MAKES: 16 OATCAKES

220g (7¾oz/2½ cups) rolled oats

65g (2¼oz/½ cup) plain (all-purpose) flour, plus extra for dusting

65g (2¼oz) cold salted butter, cubed

pinch each of sea salt and freshly ground black pepper

2 tsp dried thyme

½ tsp bicarbonate of soda (baking soda)

70ml (2⅓fl oz/⅓ cup) hot milk

Having started my baking blog and social media profile during my time living in Aberdeen, it feels crucial to include a little twist on a Scottish classic. These are a star on a cheeseboard, or to keep them really classic, serve with a lentil soup. These are super simple to make, and you can have such fun with them – I like using heart-shaped cookie cutters for a cute look!

Preheat the oven to 160°C fan (180°C/350°F/Gas 4) and line two large baking trays with baking parchment (or silicone liners).

Put all the ingredients apart from the milk in a bowl and rub together with your fingertips until the mixture forms a breadcrumb consistency. Add the hot milk and stir to form a dough (you may need a little more milk, if the texture is too dry). Tip the dough onto a floured surface and roll out to a thickness of about 5mm (¼in), then use a 6cm (2in) cookie cutter to cut about 16 oatcakes. Place the oatcakes on the lined baking trays and bake in the oven for about 20 minutes, until lightly browned at the edges.

Remove from the oven and transfer to a wire rack to cool.

The oatcakes will keep well for up to 5–7 days in an airtight container.

Easy Homemade Garlic Bread

MAKES: 4 GARLIC BREADS

1 garlic bulb

olive oil, for drizzling

100g (3½oz) salted butter, at room temperature

3 tsp finely chopped fresh parsley

sea salt and freshly ground black pepper

1 batch of 'cheats ciabatta' (page 46) or 4 store-bought ciabatta rolls

When you're craving a little garlic bread action alongside a big bowl of spaghetti, or for a sandwich, or to devour in front of the TV, there is never a bad time for garlic bread. This is really a recipe of two parts, starting with my Cheat's Ciabatta recipe (page 46), but you can use store-bought ciabatta then follow these easy steps which will have your kitchen aglow with the smell of garlic.

Preheat the oven to 160°C fan (180°C/350°F/Gas 4) and place a sheet of foil on a large baking tray.

Slice the top off the garlic bulb, place it in the middle of the foil, drizzle generously with olive oil and season well with salt. Wrap the garlic bulb in the foil to seal it and roast in the oven for about 30 minutes.

Remove from the oven, unwrap it and let it cool a few minutes, then squeeze the bulb into a bowl to release all the soft roasted garlic from their individual clove casings (pulp from their skins). Add the butter and parsley, along with some salt and pepper, and mix together to create a rich, herby, garlicky butter.

Slice your ciabattas in half and spread them with the garlic butter, then place on a baking tray in the oven for about 10 minutes until the edges are crisp and the butter has melted into the bread.

Tip
If you fancy, you can add some grated cheese after spreading the ciabattas with the garlic butter, before baking in the oven.

afternoon tea

20 mins **HANDS-ON TIME**

BAKE TIME: 15–20 MINS

TOTAL: 35–40 MINS

Rose Shortbread Cookies

MAKES: 20 COOKIES

100g (3½oz) butter, at room temperature

50g (1¾oz/4 tbsp) caster (superfine) sugar

175g (6oz/scant 1¼ cups) plain (all-purpose) flour, plus extra for dusting

1 tsp rose extract or rosewater

2 tbsp dried rose petals

To decorate

100g (3½oz) white chocolate, melted

dried rose petals, crushed

Why not try

Lavender, coconut, lemon or coffee extracts all work well in place of the rosewater. Then try topping the cookies with the respective ingredient – lavender petals, coconut flakes, lemon zest or coffee beans!

While rose may sound like an intense flavour, or bring thoughts of overpowering rosewater treats (although I personally love bright-pink Turkish delight), it can be used to create some really delicate bakes. Rosewater and rose extract are pretty easy to find now, in supermarkets and online, but bear in mind that a little goes a long way. These are such a pretty bake, perfect for setting up a classy afternoon tea situation. That said, they're also great to demolish while bingeing your favourite TV show.

Preheat the oven to 130°C fan (150°C/300°F/Gas 2) and line two large baking trays with baking parchment (or silicone liners).

Beat the butter in a large bowl for several minutes to soften – this is easiest with a stand mixer or electric handheld whisk. Add the sugar and continue to beat until fully incorporated, then add the flour, rose extract or rosewater and beat again until the mixture comes together: it should hold as a solid dough when you press it with your hands. Stir through the rose petals.

Roll out the dough onto a lightly floured surface to a thickness of 1–2cm (½–¾in), then cut out 20 rounds with a small round cookie cutter (I use a 5cm/2in cutter) and place on the lined trays – they don't need to be too spaced out as they won't spread. Bake in the oven for 15–20 minutes, until just starting to turn golden at the edges (they continue to bake a little with the residual heat after removing them from the oven).

Remove from the oven, transfer to a wire rack and leave to cool.

Once cool, dip into a bowl of melted white chocolate, just halfway, then leave to set on a wire rack and top with some crushed rose petals.

The cookies will keep well for up to 5–7 days in an airtight container.

Cherry & Almond Loaf Cake

SERVES: 8

180g (6½oz) butter, at room temperature

180g (6½oz/¾ cup) caster (superfine) sugar

3 medium eggs

2 tsp almond extract

155g (5½oz/generous 1 cup) plain (all-purpose) flour

1 tsp baking powder

5 tbsp ground almonds

3 tbsp milk

250g (9oz) pitted fresh or frozen cherries

Glaze

125g (4½oz/generous 1 cup) icing (powdered) sugar

2 tsp milk

½ tsp almond extract

To serve

3 tbsp flaked (slivered) almonds

cherries on their stem (optional)

Anything that spins off a Bakewell Tart has got to be good, right? This loaf cake brings together a terrific flavour combination of almonds and cherries and is a much easier way to recreate those beloved Bakewell flavours. The result is something perfect for afternoon tea, to cut slices off and come back to – repeatedly, no doubt.

Preheat the oven to 180°C fan (200°C/400°F/Gas 6) and line a 900g (2lb) loaf tin with baking parchment.

In a large bowl, or the bowl of a stand mixer fitted with the beater attachment, beat the butter and sugar for 3–5 minutes, until light and fluffy. Add the eggs one at a time, mixing after each addition, then add the almond extract and combine again. Combine the flour, baking powder and ground almonds then add them to the bowl and gently fold to combine. Add the milk to loosen and stir gently.

Transfer the batter into the lined tin, level it out, and bake in the oven for 50 minutes, until golden and a skewer inserted into the middle comes out clean.

Remove from the oven and leave to cool on a wire rack in the tin before turning it out and glazing it.

Make the glaze in a small bowl by combing the icing (powdered) sugar, milk and almond extract. It should be thick but pourable. Adjust if necessary. Pour the glaze over the cake and scatter over the flaked (slivered) almonds. Adding some fresh cherries, especially those still on their stems, gives a nice finishing touch.

The cake will keep well for up to 2–3 days in an airtight container.

Vegan No-bake Chocolate & Pistachio Bars (tiffin)

SERVES: 9

350g (12oz) dark chocolate, chopped

75g (2½oz) vegan butter

3 tbsp golden syrup (corn syrup) or light molasses

100g (3½oz) dried cranberries

150g (5½oz) digestive biscuits (or graham crackers), coarsely crushed

Topping

200g (7oz) dark chocolate, chopped

75g (3oz) pistachios, shelled and chopped

A tiffin is another word for fridge cake or no-bake cakes. This recipe comprises lots of melted chocolate, biscuits and fruit folded together, then left to set in the fridge before slicing. This makes it really versatile, so do play with the flavours/biscuits/add-ins. This will sit in the fridge for a few days, tempting you to come and take a piece every time you open the door!

Line a 20cm (8in) square brownie/baking tin with baking parchment.

Put the chocolate, butter and golden syrup (corn syrup) in a large heatproof bowl set over a pan of simmering water (making sure the bottom of the bowl isn't touching the water) and stir until combined and glossy.

Turn off the heat, add the cranberries and crushed biscuits to the melted chocolate mixture and stir until combined. Pour this mixture into the tin and spread it out evenly, pressing to the sides.

Make the topping: melt the dark chocolate in the microwave in 20-second intervals, stirring regularly. Once melted, pour it on top of the biscuit base. Sprinkle over the chopped pistachios. Let it set in the fridge for at least an hour (overnight is fine). Once set, cut with a hot knife for perfectly smooth slices!

The tiffin will keep well for up to 5–7 days in an airtight container in the fridge.

My All-time Favourite Lemon & Passion Fruit Cake

SERVES: 12

3 passion fruit (or use 2 tbsp coulis or sauce)

Sponge
240g (8½oz/scant 2 cups) plain (all-purpose) flour
240g (8½oz/1¼ cups) granulated sugar
2 tsp baking powder
4 large eggs
240g (8½oz) butter or margarine, at room temperature
grated zest of 1 lemon

Buttercream frosting
200g (7oz) butter, at room temperature
400g (14oz/generous 3 cups) icing (powdered) sugar
2 tbsp lemon juice
3 tbsp passion fruit coulis or sauce
grated zest of 1 lemon

This all-in-one fluffy cake recipe topped with the most luscious lemon and passion fruit buttercream is moist and zesty and everything that you want a lemon cake to be. If you can't find fresh passion fruits, use passion fruit coulis or sauce, which can usually be found in baking aisles in larger supermarkets. This is vibrant and truly so easy to make!

Preheat the oven to 160°C fan (180°C/350°F/Gas 4) and line 2 x 20cm (8in) round cake tins with baking parchment.

Cut the passion fruit in half, scooping out the fruit inside and strain over a bowl to get the juice. Set aside, keeping the seeds and fruit fibres in another bowl for later.

In a large bowl, or the bowl of a stand mixer fitted with the beater attachment, add all the sponge ingredients, including the strained passion fruit juice, and combine until smooth. If very stiff, add a little milk. Divide evenly between the two lined tins, level out, and bake in the oven for 20–25 minutes, until golden and a skewer inserted into each cake comes out clean.

Remove from the oven and leave to cool in the tins on a wire rack.

Once cool, make the buttercream. Put the butter in a large bowl and beat with an electric whisk on high speed for a minute to soften. Add half the icing (powdered) sugar and whisk on high until incorporated, then add the lemon juice and the remaining icing sugar and whisk on high until fluffy. Add a little milk or more icing sugar as required, until it reaches your desired consistency.

Spread the buttercream over one of the cakes and add the coulis to the very middle of the cake, not spreading it to the edges. Top with the other cake and cover with buttercream. Decorate with the lemon zest and the remaining passion fruit flesh and seeds (or coulis/sauce), as desired.

The cake will keep well for up to 3 days in the fridge in an airtight container.

Spiced Ginger Traybake

SERVES: 9

170g (5¾oz/generous 1 cup) plain (all-purpose) flour

1 tbsp ground ginger

1 tbsp ground cinnamon

1 tsp ground mixed spice

1 tsp bicarbonate of soda (baking soda)

80g (2¾oz) butter

95g (31/3 oz/½ cup) soft dark brown sugar

70g (2½oz) golden syrup (corn syrup)

80g (2¾oz) black treacle (molasses)

2 tbsp milk

1 egg, beaten

Glaze

75g (2½oz) icing (powdered) sugar

1½ tbsp milk

30g (1oz) stem ginger from a jar, chopped (I chop it coarsely, but finely works too)

The perfect nostalgic British bake. I think some people view ginger cake as a little old-fashioned, but I think it fits in fabulously well at an afternoon tea table, or gobbled up over the kitchen counter while having a chat with a friend (who, me? Guilty as charged). The glaze and the chopped stem ginger decor add a little more sweetness and spice, which gives it a bit of extra spark.

Preheat the oven to 170°C fan (190°C/370°F/Gas 5) and line a 20cm (8in) square brownie/baking/cake tin with baking parchment.

In a large bowl, or the bowl of a stand mixer fitted with the beater attachment, combine the flour, dried spices and bicarbonate of soda (baking soda).

Put the butter, brown sugar, golden syrup (corn syrup) and treacle (molasses) in a medium saucepan and heat over a low heat until melted, keeping an eye on it. Once it's all melted, add the liquid to the dry ingredients, add the milk and mix until combined (on medium speed if you're using a stand mixer). Add the egg and mix again.

Pour the batter into the lined tin or tray, level it out, and bake in the oven for 30–35 minutes, until a skewer inserted into the middle comes out clean.

Remove from the oven and leave to cool on a wire rack.

Once the cake has cooled, make the glaze by combining the icing (powdered) sugar and milk. Pour this over the top of the cake (while it's still in the tin or tray) and scatter over the chopped stem ginger. Leave to set, then cut and serve.

The traybake will keep well for up to 4 days in an airtight container.

BAKE TIME: 35 MINS

COOLING TIME: AT LEAST 1 HR

TOTAL: 1 HR 55 MINS

White Chocolate Ganache-frosted Loaf Cake

SERVES: 8

180g (6½oz/scant 1⅓ cups) plain (all-purpose) flour

1 tsp baking powder

1 tsp bicarbonate of soda (baking soda)

160g (5½oz/¾ cup) granulated sugar

pinch of fine sea salt

2 medium eggs

2 tbsp golden syrup (corn syrup)

150ml (5fl oz/⅔ cup) vegetable oil

2 tsp vanilla extract

160ml (5½fl oz/⅔ cup) milk

100g (3½oz) white chocolate chips (or coarsely chopped white chocolate)

Ganache frosting

100g (3½oz) white chocolate, finely chopped

150ml (5fl oz/⅔ cup) double (heavy) cream

Before anyone starts telling me 'white chocolate isn't real chocolate', my response is that I simply don't care. There is something so luscious about white chocolate! So, turning it into whipped ganache just made sense to me. This is easier than it may sound, and provides a great alternative to a classic buttercream-style frosting. Upon serving this, do expect to cut repeatedly as it is devilishly moreish!

Preheat the oven to 180°C fan (200°C/400°F/Gas 6) and line a 900g (2lb) loaf tin with baking parchment.

In a large bowl, or the bowl of a stand mixer fitted with the beater attachment, combine the flour, baking powder, bicarbonate of soda (baking soda), sugar and salt. Whisk the eggs, syrup, oil, vanilla extract and milk in a jug then make a well in the dry mixture, pour in the mixture from the jug and stir to combine. Fold through the chocolate chips.

Transfer the batter into the lined tin, level it out, and bake in the oven for 35 minutes, until a skewer inserted into the middle of the cake comes out clean.

Remove from the oven and leave to cool on a wire rack.

While the cake cools, make the frosting (as it needs time to cool before whisking). Put the chopped chocolate in a heatproof bowl. Heat the cream in a pan over a low heat, until it just starts to bubble, then pour it over the chopped chocolate and leave for 2 minutes. Stir together until a gorgeously shiny chocolate ganache forms. Leave to cool for at least 1 hour.

Put the cooled chocolate ganache in the bowl of a stand mixer fitted with the whisk attachment, or a bowl that you can use an electric handheld whisk in, and whisk on a high speed for 2–3 minutes, until light and fluffy. Spread this over the top of the cake, adding any sprinkles/decorations you like. Serve as soon as you can!

The cake will keep well for up to 3 days in an airtight container in the fridge.

CHILL TIME: 30 MINS

BAKE TIME: 50–60 MINS

TOTAL: 1 HR 55–2 HRS 5 MINS

Lemon & Blueberry Bakewell Tart

SERVES: 8

Shortcrust pastry (makes about 320g/11¼oz)

220g (7¾oz) cold butter, cubed, plus extra for greasing

100g (3½oz/⅔ cup) plain (all-purpose) flour, plus extra for dusting

3 tsp cold water

1 medium egg, beaten

Frangipane tart

200g (7oz) lemon curd

175g (6oz) butter, at room temperature

175g (6oz/generous ¾ cup) granulated sugar

3 medium eggs

1 tsp almond extract

175g (6oz/1½ cups) ground almonds

1 tbsp grated lemon zest

150g (5½oz) blueberries

1 tbsp plain (all-purpose) flour

handful of flaked (slivered) almonds

Glaze

6 tbsp icing (powdered) sugar

1 tbsp milk

Lashings of lemon curd and fresh blueberries replace the classic cherry flavouring in this twist on a British staple. Perfect to impress your friends at a home-hosted afternoon tea. A food processor creates a really quick shortcrust pastry, but store-bought pastry is totally fine as always. I like to think of this as the perfect summer dessert, full of happy, fresh flavours.

Start by making the pastry, if making your own. Put the butter and flour in a bowl and rub them together with your fingertips until the texture resembles breadcrumbs (or use a food processor to do this), then add the water until a dough forms. Form the dough into a ball, flatten slightly, wrap the dough in cling film (plastic wrap) and chill in the fridge for 15 minutes.

Preheat the oven to 170°C fan (190°C/370°F/Gas 5) and lightly grease a 23cm (9in) loose-bottomed tart tin with butter.

Unwrap the pastry and roll it out on a floured surface to a thickness of 5mm (¼in), so it's large enough to line the tin. Press it into the tart tin, pushing it into the edges, then cut off any excess around the rim. Place a circle of baking parchment on top of the pastry – enough to go up the sides – fill with baking beans or raw rice so that the base is entirely covered and weighed down, and bake blind for 10 minutes.

Remove the tin from the oven, carefully remove the paper and the beans or rice, then brush with the beaten egg and bake for a further 5–10 minutes, until the pastry is just cooked and lightly golden.

Remove from the oven and let the pastry cool for at least 15 minutes, then spread over the lemon curd.

continued overleaf

To make the frangipane batter, first mix the butter and sugar on high speed with an electric handheld whisk (or a stand mixer fitted with the whisk attachment) for 3–5 minutes until light and fluffy. Add the eggs and almond extract, then gently fold in the ground almonds and lemon zest. Coat the blueberries in the flour (to stop them sinking), then gently fold them into the batter.

Pour this batter over the lemon curd-covered pastry base. Sprinkle over some flaked (slivered) almonds and bake the tart in the oven for 35–40 minutes, until golden on top.

Remove from the oven and leave to cool on a wire rack.

Make the glaze once the tart has cooled by combining the icing (powdered) sugar and milk and drizzling it over the tart. Slice and serve.

Tip

The topping can sometimes start to brown before the filling is entirely cooked. If you find this happening, move the tart to the bottom shelf of your oven, and 'tent' it by covering the top loosely in foil while it continues to bake.

Chocolate Fudge Cupcakes

MAKES: 6 CUPCAKES

110g (3¾oz) butter, at room temperature

110g (3¾oz/½ cup) granulated sugar

2 medium eggs

1 tsp vanilla extract

110g (3¾oz/generous ⅔ cup) plain (all-purpose) flour

1 tsp baking powder

2 tbsp cocoa powder

1 tsp instant coffee powder

2 tbsp milk

Buttercream frosting

180g (6½oz) butter, at room temperature

380g (13½oz/3 cups) icing (powdered) sugar

40g (1½oz) dark chocolate, melted

1 tbsp cocoa powder

chocolate sprinkles (optional)

Decadent chocolate cupcakes topped with a chocolate fudge buttercream frosting – need I go into further detail? This is THE bake for chocolate lovers, and they travel well for birthday parties or gifts!

Preheat the oven to 180°C fan (200°C/400°F/Gas 6) and line a 6-hole muffin tin (pan) with paper cases.

In a large bowl, or the bowl of a stand mixer fitted with the beater attachment, beat the butter and sugar for 3–5 minutes on high speed until light and fluffy. Add the eggs, one at a time, mixing after each addition, then add the vanilla extract. Combine the flour, baking powder, cocoa powder and instant coffee, gently fold them into the wet mixture until just combined, then add the milk to loosen the batter a little.

Scoop the batter evenly into the muffin tin cases: they should be about two-thirds full. Bake in the oven for 18–20 minutes, until a skewer inserted into one of the cakes comes out clean.

Remove from the oven and leave to cool on a wire rack.

Once cool, make the buttercream. Put the butter and half the icing (powdered) sugar in a bowl and beat on high speed with an electric mixer. Once combined, add the melted chocolate, cocoa powder and the rest of the icing sugar and beat until smooth and fluffy. Pipe or spread onto the cooled cupcakes and top with sprinkles (if using).

The cupcakes will keep well for up to 3 days in an airtight container.

Rhubarb & Custard Shortcake Stacks

SERVES: 4

Pastry

200g (7oz/1½ cups) plain (all-purpose) flour, plus extra for dusting

2 tsp baking powder

45g (1½oz/3½ tbsp) granulated sugar

pinch of fine sea salt

70g (2½oz) cold butter, cubed

60ml (2fl oz/¼ cup) milk

60ml (2fl oz/¼ cup) double (heavy) cream

Filling

350g (12oz) rhubarb, cut into 1cm (½in)-thick slices

85g (3oz/⅓ cup) granulated sugar

500g (1lb 2oz) store-bought fresh/chilled custard, plus extra to serve

icing (powdered) sugar, for dusting

Juicy stewed rhubarb and fresh custard give these shortcake stacks the most gorgeous colour. So photogenic, and so fun to throw together, they are sure to brighten up your table. The shortcakes get baked before being sliced in half and filled with the custard and rhubarb.

Line a large baking tray with baking parchment.

Combine the flour, baking powder, sugar and salt in a large bowl, add the butter and rub together with your fingertips until the mixture forms a pebble-like texture. Pour in the milk and cream and bring everything together with a knife. Tip the dough onto a floured surface and divide into 4 large equal-sized pieces. Form into rounds about 7.5cm (3in) in diameter, rolling them out then shaping them with your hands, place on tray and chill in the fridge for 15 minutes. Preheat the oven to 200°C fan (220°C/430°F/Gas 7).

Bake the chilled pastry rounds in the oven for 25 minutes, until golden. While the pastry is baking, put the sliced rhubarb in a small saucepan with the sugar and a splash of water and simmer for about 10 minutes, until the rhubarb has softened. Set aside.

Once the shortcakes have baked, leave to cool a little on a wire rack. Once cool, assemble the shortbreads: slice the shortcakes in half widthways, layer up the warm rhubarb and ready-made custard on the base, then top with the shortcake 'lid'. Serve with a dusting of icing (powdered) sugar and extra custard on the side.

The unfilled shortbreads will keep well for up to 4 days in an airtight container.

Why not try

1. The classic, with strawberries and whipped cream

2. Cinnamon apples with caramel sauce

3. Stewed cranberries with orange zest and brandy cream

Chocolate Coconut Cake

SERVES: 10

350g (12oz/2¾ cups) plain (all-purpose) flour

2 tsp baking powder

2 tsp bicarbonate of soda (baking soda)

35g (1¼oz) cocoa powder

300g (10½oz/1½ cups) granulated sugar

4 large eggs

4 tbsp golden syrup, honey, light molasses or light corn syrup

300ml (10fl oz/1⅓ cups) vegetable oil

200ml (7fl oz/scant 1 cup) coconut milk

120ml (4fl oz/½ cup) milk

Buttercream frosting

200g (7oz) butter, at room temperature

500g (1lb 2oz/5 cups) icing (powdered) sugar

50ml (1¾fl oz/3½ tbsp) coconut milk

To finish

coconut flakes, for sprinkling

Like a Bounty chocolate bar turned into a layered cake, this is a real centrepiece bake, that can be dressed up or down as much as you like. The sponge is moist and decadent, just how a chocolate cake should be, and the buttercream frosting brings in the real coconut element with just a little texture which gives this cake the wow factor.

Preheat the oven to 180°C fan (200°C/400°F/Gas 6) and line 2 x 20cm (8in) round cake tins with baking parchment.

In a large bowl, or the bowl of a stand mixer fitted with the beater attachment, combine the flour, baking powder, bicarbonate of soda (baking soda), cocoa powder and sugar. Make a well in the dry mixture and add the eggs, syrup and oil. Mix thoroughly, then pour in both the milks and mix again until incorporated. The batter will be fairly runny.

Divide the batter evenly between the lined tins, level it out, and bake in the oven for 35 minutes, until a skewer inserted into the middle of each cake comes out clean.

Remove from the oven and leave to cool in the tins on a wire rack. If the cakes are very domed, you may want to cut off the tops once they're cool and you've removed them from their tins so they can sit flat.

Once cool, make the buttercream: beat the butter on high speed with an electric handheld whisk or the bowl of a stand mixer fitted with the whisk attachment, then add half the icing (powdered) sugar and all of the coconut milk and continue mixing for several minutes until combined. Add the remaining icing sugar and beat until the buttercream has the desired consistency.

continued overleaf

Now layer up the cakes: place one cake on a board, top it with about half of the buttercream and spread it out evenly. Place the other cake upside down on top and spread with the remaining buttercream. Sprinkle the coconut flakes around the edge.

The cake will keep well for up to 3 days in an airtight container in the fridge.

Why not try

1. For a simpler cake, halve the recipe to make a single cake, and top with whipped cream and some extra coconut!

2. To dress it up, make double the buttercream to entirely coat the cake and create a ring around the top with extra piped frosting. Press on toasted coconut flakes, or coconut truffles!

Mini Piña Colada Loaf Cakes

MAKES: 8 MINI LOAF CAKES

100g (3½oz) butter, at room temperature

165g (5¾oz/¾ cup) granulated sugar

3 medium eggs

1 tsp orange extract (optional)

3½ tbsp pineapple juice (from a tin or carton)

255g (9oz/scant 2 cups) plain (all-purpose) flour

½ tsp bicarbonate of soda (baking soda)

1½ tsp baking powder

215ml (7¼fl oz/scant 1 cup) chilled coconut milk (from a tin), or regular whole milk

Buttercream frosting

120g (4¼oz) butter, at room temperature

2 tbsp pineapple juice

2 tbsp rum or coconut rum (or more pineapple juice if you prefer)

280g (10oz/2½ cups) icing (powdered) sugar

desiccated (shredded) coconut or coconut flakes, to decorate

For those who lean towards fruity cakes as opposed to chocolate, these coconut cakes are a teatime delight. Mini loaf tins tend to be pretty easy to come across now, with major supermarkets often stocking them. The rum is totally optional!

Preheat the oven to 180°C fan (200°C/400°F/Gas 6) and line 8 mini loaf tins with baking parchment (the tins I use are about 8.5 x 6.5cm/3.5 x 2.5in).

In a large bowl, or the bowl of a stand mixer fitted with the beater attachment, mix the butter and granulated sugar for 3–5 minutes until light and fluffy. Add the eggs, one at a time, beating after each addition, then add the orange extract (if using). Add the pineapple juice and combine again. The mixture may begin to look a little curdled but stick with it!

Mix together the flour, bicarbonate of soda (baking soda) and baking powder in a small bowl. Add a third to the butter/egg/juice mix, plus a third of the coconut milk, and mix until combined. Repeat with the remaining flour mix and milk. The mixture will be fairly smooth and should pour easily.

Pour the batter evenly into the tins and bake in the oven for 20–25 minutes, until a skewer inserted into the middle of one of the cakes comes out clean.

Remove from the oven and leave to cool in the tins on a wire rack.

Once cool, make the buttercream: whisk the butter on high speed with an electric mixer, then add the pineapple juice and rum (if using, otherwise use an additional 2 tbsp pineapple juice) and half the icing (powdered) sugar. Mix on high until the sugar is incorporated, then add the rest of the sugar. Mix until everything comes together in glorious golden waves, ensuring the buttercream is thick enough to spread – if not, add more icing sugar. Spread this over the cakes and decorate with desiccated coconut or toasted coconut flakes.

The cakes will keep well for up to 3 days in an airtight container in the fridge.

Tip

The key to lining the tins is to cut strips of baking parchment that are long enough to run over the top edges, so you can essentially lift the cakes out using the parchment ends as 'tabs'. Cut the parchment the way you would for a loaf tin – so it isn't covering all four sides, but just the two longest and make sure there is a lot of overhang so you can lift the cakes up (see photo page 100–101). If unclear, check out my Instagram or website for mini loaf cakes that use this lining method.

Gooey Raspberry Cake

SERVES: 8

120g (4¼oz) butter, melted, plus extra for greasing

165g (5¾oz/¾ cup) granulated sugar

1 medium egg

2 tbsp milk

170g (5¾oz/generous 1 cup) plain (all-purpose) flour

1 tsp baking powder

Topping

180g (6½oz) full-fat cream cheese

1 medium egg

400g (14oz/generous 3 cups) icing (powdered) sugar, plus extra for dusting

150g (5½oz) raspberries

A classic, gorgeously moist sponge, covered with a small mountain of raspberries and a slightly crisp, but super gooey topping: the result is a marriage of really happy flavours and textures. Cosy and comforting in all the right ways.

Preheat the oven to 180°C fan (200°C/400°F/Gas 6) and grease a 23cm (9in) round cake tin with butter (I use one with a removable base for extra ease when it comes to turning out the cake).

In a large bowl, or the bowl of a stand mixer fitted with the beater attachment, combine the melted butter and sugar for about 3 minutes until well mixed. Add the egg and milk and mix again. Fold in the flour and baking powder to form a loose cake batter, pour this into the lined tin and use a spatula to spread it out evenly. Set aside.

To make the topping, beat all ingredients apart from the berries together in a large bowl. This should form a creamy, runny mixture. Gently pour this over the cake batter, spreading it out to the edges, scatter over the raspberries and bake in the oven for 40–45 minutes, checking on it at about 30 minutes to ensure it isn't burning at the edges. If it gets too golden/dark, cover with foil for the remaining bake time. It should only have a very small 'wobble' when it is ready.

Remove from the oven and leave to cool on a wire rack. Dust with icing (powdered) sugar and serve! Whipped cream makes a great accompaniment.

The cake will keep well for up to 3 days in an airtight container.

Marble Coffee Cake

BAKE TIME: 50 MINS–1 HOUR

TOTAL: 1 HR 10 MINS–1 HR 20 MINS

SERVES: 8

180g (6½oz) butter, at room temperature

180g (6½oz/¾ cup) granulated sugar

3 medium eggs

180g (6½oz/scant 1⅓ cups) plain (all-purpose) flour

1½ tsp baking powder

2 tbsp milk

1 tbsp cocoa powder

1 tbsp instant coffee dissolved in 20ml water (or ½ shot of espresso)

Tip

For successful marbling, blob the different batters one by one, making sure there is some definition. When swirling, only do so a little, so that there are still clear separate colours. If you swirl too much, the colours just mix into one batter! Using a knife works well as it's quite a loose mixture.

Giving major mocha vibes, this loaf cake has swirls of coffee and chocolate throughout. Marble cake has always been the go-to cake for my dad's birthday, and it's an easy winner to have on hand if you're hosting people or want to have something ready to snack on.

Preheat the oven to 160°C fan (180°C/350°F/Gas 4) and line a 900g (2lb) loaf tin with baking parchment.

In a large bowl with an electric whisk, or the bowl of a stand mixer fitted with the beater attachment, beat the butter and sugar for 3–5 minutes until light and fluffy. Add the eggs one at a time, mixing after each addition, until well incorporated, then combine the flour and baking powder and gently fold them into the wet mixture. Add about half of the milk – you want the batter to be smooth and pourable but not really runny (add more milk if necessary).

Scoop half the batter into another bowl. In this bowl, add the cocoa powder and coffee and mix.

Add large tablespoons of each batter to the lined tin, one at a time, so that there are 'scoops' of the vanilla and chocolate/coffee cake. Repeat until all the batter is used up, then swirl lightly with a knife (taking care not to mix the batters together too much – you want them to remain distinct) then bake in the oven for 50 minutes to 1 hour, until golden on top and a knife, when inserted, comes out clean.

Remove from the oven and leave to cool in the tin on a wire rack before serving.

The cake will keep well for up to 4 days in an airtight container.

Orange Drizzle Scones

MAKES: 6 SCONES

250g (9oz/scant 2 cups) plain (all-purpose) flour

3 tbsp granulated sugar

2 tsp baking powder

130g (4½oz) cold salted butter, cubed

80ml (2¾fl oz/⅓ cup) milk

grated zest of 1 orange

1 medium egg, beaten

Drizzle

juice of 1 orange

75g (2½oz/⅓ cup) granulated sugar

Glaze

3 tbsp icing (powdered) sugar

squeeze of orange juice

These fluffy, zesty scones are covered with an orange drizzle and extra orange drizzle icing, making them the perfect light scone full of fresh zingy flavour. A little twist on a classic, these are super fragrant and I love making them in the summer, when they make a change from all the chocolate I use through the rest of the year.

Preheat the oven to 190°C fan (210°C/410°F/Gas 7) and line a large baking tray with baking parchment (or a silicone liner).

In a food processor, or using your hands, combine the flour, sugar and baking powder. Add the butter and rub it in (or blitz), until the mixture resembles breadcrumbs. Add the milk and grated orange zest and use a knife to combine until the mixture forms a shaggy dough (if you're using a food processor, remove the blade and do this in the processor bowl).

Tip the mixture onto a baking tray and shape it into a circle about 15cm (6in) wide and 2.5cm (1in) thick. Score 5mm (¼in)-deep lines to mark where you will cut them once baked (I divide the dough into 6 triangles – pizza-style). Brush with the beaten egg and bake in the oven for about 15 minutes, until golden brown.

Remove from the oven and use a sharp knife to split the scones into the triangles you scored earlier (do this while they're still warm).

Combine the orange juice and the sugar for the drizzle mixture and pour this over each scone. Leave to cool on a wire rack.

Once cool, make the glaze. Combine the icing (powdered) sugar and orange juice to create a runny glaze and drizzle it over each scone. Serve once this has set.

The scones will keep well for up to 2 days in an airtight container.

15 mins **HANDS-ON TIME**

FRY TIME: 10 MINS

TOTAL: 25 MINS

Sugared Donut Holes

MAKES: ABOUT 20 DONUT HOLES

1 litre (34fl oz/4¼ cups) vegetable oil (any light/non-flavoured oil), for deep frying

240ml (8fl oz/1 cup) milk

1 large egg

65g (2¼oz) butter, melted

240g (8½oz/scant 2 cups) plain (all-purpose) flour

2 tsp baking powder

pinch of fine sea salt

100g (3½oz/½ cup) granulated sugar, to coat, plus 3 tbsp for the dough

These small balls of dough that get fried and covered in sugar are baby-sized bites of donut – think funfair-style donuts. Deep frying isn't something I do often, but this is one of those recipes that is SO worth it! Top with heaps of granulated sugar for that beautiful first bite. I'm slightly cheating as there is no yeast involved, but that results in a much faster recipe!

Line a large baking tray with some kitchen paper – this is for draining the excess fat from the fried donuts.

Heat the oil in a large saucepan – you want it to be at least 5cm (2in) deep. If you have a thermometer, the oil needs to reach 180°C (350°F), but don't worry if you don't.

While the oil heats up, put the milk, egg and melted butter in a large bowl and whisk to combine. Whisk in the flour, baking powder, salt and 3 tablespoons of sugar until a thick batter forms.

To test the oil is ready, take a tiny amount of the dough (about ½ a teaspoon) and drop it into the oil. If the oil bubbles immediately, it's ready!

Use a tablespoon to scoop balls of batter and gently drop them into the oil (the oil is HOT so be really careful). They will expand as they fry, so take care not to overcrowd the pan. Fry for 2 minutes or so, then flip and cook for another minute or two until golden.

Remove with a slotted spoon and place on the paper-lined tray and continue frying the rest of the batter.

While still warm, roll the donut holes in a bowl of granulated sugar, then eat at your pleasure – they are great warm or when cool!

Tip
Try dusting the fried dough with 1 tsp ground cinnamon combined with the sugar for a churro vibe.

Cinnamon Sugar Popovers with Warm Honey

MAKES: 6 POPOVERS

70g (2½oz/½ cup) plain (all-purpose) flour

2 large eggs

1 tsp vanilla extract

100ml (3½fl oz/scant ½ cup) milk

6 tsp vegetable oil

2 tbsp honey

Cinnamon sugar

30g (1oz) granulated sugar

1 tsp ground cinnamon

Popovers are made with a batter not unlike pancake/Yorkshire pudding batter. These are definitely best served warm, and can get a little messy if you're anything like me. Tearing apart the flaky dough (is it technically dough? I don't know, but it's delicious) and mopping up the warm honey is the ideal way to spend your time.

Make the batter by whisking the flour, eggs, vanilla extract and milk in a large jug until no lumps remain. Chill for at least 20 minutes (this isn't critical, but I highly recommend it).

Preheat the oven to 210°C fan (230°C/450°F/Gas 8).

Pour 1 teaspoon of vegetable oil into each hole of a 6-hole muffin tin (pan). Place in the oven to get the oil hot.

Once the batter has chilled, remove it from the fridge, remove the tin from the oven and pour the batter directly into each muffin hole. Bake in the oven for 20–25 minutes, until the popovers are golden brown and really puffed up.

Remove from the oven and place on a wire rack.

Mix together the sugar and cinnamon in a large, shallow bowl.

After the popovers have cooled for a few minutes, remove from the tin and dip each popover into the cinnamon sugar mixture. Drizzle warm honey (give it a 10- or 20-second blast in the microwave) over the top and serve immediately!

after-dinner desserts

Husband Tart

SERVES: 10

Base

300g (10½oz) Oreo cookies

100g (3½oz) butter, melted

Ganache filling

200g (7oz) dark chocolate, finely chopped

100g (3½oz) milk chocolate, finely chopped

150ml (5fl oz/⅔ cup) double (heavy) cream

75g (2½oz) butter

100g (3½oz) raspberries

To finish

150ml (5fl oz/⅔ cup) double (heavy) cream

raspberries

dark chocolate shavings

My ultimate no-bake chocolate and raspberry tart. The name came from my partner and biggest advocate who, after a serious WOW moment, proclaimed this was the best thing I had ever made, closely followed by 'You should name this husband tart, the upgrade from boyfriend cookies' (more on those in the final chapter). This is made up of an Oreo cookie base, chocolate ganache, raspberries, topped with whipped cream. Not only is it delicious, but it looks stunning, and is a wonderful way to end Sunday lunch or a dinner party. The best part? You'll be stunned how easy it is to pull together, perfect to prompt that awaited proposal.

First, make the base. Blitz the Oreos in a food processor or bash them with a rolling pin (in a sealed plastic bag or bowl) until they form fine crumbs. Add the melted butter and stir together. Press into a 23cm (9in) tart tin (a loose-bottomed one works great here, and I use one that's got a fluted edge), making sure it comes up the sides of the tin, and set aside.

Now make the ganache. Put the chopped chocolate in a large heatproof bowl. Put the cream and butter in a small saucepan and heat over a low heat until the butter has melted and the cream is beginning to bubble around the edges. Immediately pour it over the chocolate and leave for 2 minutes before stirring with a spatula; it might look odd to begin with but in seconds it will transform into a glossy chocolate ganache.

Sprinkle the raspberries over the tart base, then pour over the ganache and spread it out evenly. Chill in the fridge for 1 hour (this can now sit overnight or until ready to serve).

The tart will keep well for up to 3 days in an airtight container in the fridge.

Whip the cream using a handheld or manual whisk until soft peaks form, then spread the cream over the tart, adding extra raspberries and chocolate shavings (simply grate chocolate on a fine cheese grater). Serve!

Mini Biscoff Cheesecake Jars

SERVES: 4

Base

170g (5¾oz) Biscoff (Speculoos) biscuits

75g (2½oz) butter, melted

Topping

190ml (7fl oz/scant 1 cup) double (heavy) cream

70g (2½oz/generous ½ cup) icing (powdered) sugar

400g (14oz) full-fat cream cheese

3 tbsp Biscoff (cookie butter) spread

crushed Biscoff (cookie butter) biscuits, to decorate

If you're in search of an easy, no-bake, make-ahead dessert, then this is it! These look fabulous served up after dinner with friends. The combination of Biscoff (Speculoos) with the lightly whipped cheesecake results in just the right thing to round off a meal. You can use any sort of jar or short tumbler style glass.

Crush the biscuits using a food processor or by putting the biscuits into a bowl and bashing with a rolling pin until they form fine crumbs. Stir in the melted butter. Press this mixture into four glass jars/ramekins to form the base and put in the fridge while you make the topping.

Pour the double (heavy) cream into a large bowl and whisk until soft peaks form.

In a separate bowl, whisk the icing (powdered) sugar and cream cheese until fully combined. It may go runny before thickening, but that's fine. Fold the whipped cream into the cream cheese mixture. Spoon this topping over the bases and level the mixture to create a neat layer.

Loosen the Biscoff spread by heating it in a small bowl in the microwave for 30 seconds. Pour it over each of the cheesecakes to form the topping, decorate with some crushed biscuits and chill for at least 45 minutes before serving.

The jars will keep well for up to 3 days in the fridge (without the biscuit decoration).

Lattice-topped Cherry & Strawberry Pie

SERVES: 8

Shortcrust pastry

110g (3¾oz/generous ⅔ cup) plain (all-purpose) flour, plus extra for dusting

55g (2oz) cold butter, cubed, plus extra for greasing

2–4 tbsp cold water

1 medium egg, beaten

Filling

700g (1lb 9oz) pitted cherries, coarsely chopped (fresh or frozen)

2 tsp vanilla extract

150g (5½oz/¾ cup) granulated sugar, plus extra for sprinkling

2 tbsp lemon juice

2 tbsp cornflour (cornstarch)

200g (7oz) strawberry jam

Cherry pie was one of my top requests as a child/teenager, with a request for cherry pie in place of birthday cake one year... To say this is one of my 'death row' dessert options would be an understatement. This is a bit of a cheat version, as I don't use a pastry base, which would add time to the process, just a lattice pastry top. I recommend serving it hot with a heap of good-quality vanilla ice cream – the lack of base means it is best served as a warm bowl dessert!

Combine the butter and flour by rubbing them together with your fingertips in a bowl until the mixture resembles breadcrumbs (you could use a food processor for this). Add 2 tablespoons of cold water and combine again. If mixture is still dry and not coming together, add 2 more tablespoons of cold water and bring together until a dough forms. Form into a ball, flatten slightly, wrap in cling film (plastic wrap) and chill in the fridge for 15 minutes while you prepare the filling.

Preheat the oven to 180°C fan (200°C/400°F/Gas 6) and grease a 18cm (7in) pie dish with a little butter.

To make the filling, combine the chopped cherries, vanilla extract, sugar, lemon juice and cornflour (cornstarch) in a saucepan over a medium heat and cook for about 5 minutes to start to soften the cherries. Stir through the jam and tip into the pie dish.

Roll out the pastry on a floured surface to a thickness of about 1cm (½in) then cut it into long strips. Dampen the edge of the pie dish with a little water and stick some strips around the edge, then arrange the strips over the filling in the pie dish in a cross-hatch so they are equal distance apart, with the same number of strips going vertical as horizontal, weaving them over and under each other to form a lattice, attach to the pastry edge with a little water so it sticks.

Brush the beaten egg over the pastry strips, sprinkle the strips with some sugar and put the dish on a baking tray. Bake in the oven for 20 minutes, reduce the oven temperature to 160°C fan (180°C/350°F/Gas 4) and cook for a further 20–25 minutes. Remove and let it cool a little before serving. The filling will ooze, so I recommend using a spoon to serve it!

Strawberry & Cream Puffs

MAKES: 12 PUFFS

350g (12oz) store-bought all-butter puff pastry (or use my rough puff pastry on page 52)

a little flour, for dusting

1 medium egg, beaten, for brushing

1½ tbsp milk (optional)

a little granulated sugar, for sprinkling

600ml (20fl oz/2½ cups) double (heavy) cream

jar of strawberry jam

500g (18oz/2½ cups) fresh strawberries, sliced

icing (powdered) sugar, for dusting (optional)

Tip

If you are making this recipe ahead of time, make the pastry the night before but avoid filling it until the last minute. The pastry gets soggy/sad if left too long once filled.

This is an ode to my mum and a nod to a classic and a super simple recipe that feels called for when it's too warm and sunny outside to be standing around in the kitchen. There is so much I could say about the happy memories I have connected to these little bakes! Simply put, these puffs consist of flaky pastry, jam and cream assembled in a sort of sandwich style: they are not at all fussy and can be pulled together with just basic ingredients.

Preheat the oven to 180°C fan (200°C/400°F/Gas 6) and line two large baking trays with baking parchment.

Roll out the puff pastry on a floured surface to a thickness of about 5mm (¼in) – you'll be splitting it into layers once baked.

Slice the pastry into twelve 7.5 x 10cm (3 x 4in) rectangles, trying to keep them fairly even, then place them spaced apart on the lined baking trays (you may need to bake the rectangles in batches). Mix the beaten egg with the milk then, if using pre-made puff pastry, brush the pastry rectangles with the egg mix and sprinkle with granulated sugar. Bake in the oven for 10–12 minutes, until just golden, then remove and leave to cool.

Once the pastry's cool, whisk the cream until soft peaks form, by hand or with an electric handheld whisk. Take care if using an electric whisk, as it's easy to overwhip the cream. Set aside.

Pull open the cooled puff pastry rectangles along the long side of the rectangle to split them in half: the top and bottom part should be separated. Spread a teaspoon of jam along the inside of one half, and top with sliced strawberries, a good spoon of whipped cream on the other then more strawberries, before sandwiching together. Dust over some sifted icing (powdered) sugar, if liked and serve immediately!

HANDS-ON TIME

BAKE TIME: 15–25 MINS

CHILL TIME: 15 MINS

TOTAL: 1 HR 10 MINS–1 HR 20 MINS

Chocolate Tart with Hazelnut Praline

SERVES: 10

Shortcrust pastry (makes 320g/11¼oz)

100g (3½oz) cold butter, plus extra for greasing

220g (7¾oz/generous 1½ cups) plain (all-purpose) flour, plus extra for dusting

3 tbsp cold water

Praline

100g (3½oz) hazelnuts (skin-on)

225g (8oz/1 cup) granulated sugar

½ tbsp butter

Ganache filling

200g (7oz) dark chocolate, finely chopped

100g (3½oz) milk chocolate, finely chopped

150ml (5fl oz/⅔ cup) double (heavy) cream

75g (2½oz) butter

A light, crisp pastry encasing a rich chocolate ganache filling, topped with a hazelnut praline – this is a real showstopper. Don't be afraid to work with the hot sugar; I go through it in easy steps! Feel free to use store-bought pastry if you prefer not to make your own.

Start by making the pastry, if making your own. Put the butter and flour in a bowl and rub them together with your fingertips until the texture resembles breadcrumbs (alternatively, this can be done in a food processor). Add the water a little at a time until a dough forms. Shape into a ball, flatten slightly, wrap in cling film (plastic wrap) and chill in the fridge for 15 minutes.

Preheat the oven to 180°C fan (200°C/400°F/Gas 6) and lightly grease a 23cm (9in) loose-bottomed tart tin with butter (I like to use a fluted tin but any will do).

Unwrap the pastry and roll it out on a floured surface to a thickness of 5mm (¼in), until it's large enough to line the tin. Press it into the tin, right up to the edges, and cut off any excess around the rim. Line the pastry with a sheet of paking parchment – enough to go up the sides – fill it with baking beans or raw rice so that the base is entirely covered and weighed down, then bake in the oven for 10 minutes, before carefully removing the paper/beans/rice and baking for a further 5–15 minutes, until the pastry is just cooked and golden.

While the pastry is baking, put the hazelnuts on a baking tray and toast for 10 minutes.

Remove the baked pastry shell from the oven and leave to cool on a wire rack.

Put the chopped chocolate in a heatproof bowl. Heat the cream and butter in a small saucepan over a very low heat, until the butter has melted and bubbles are just forming at the edges. Pour this over the chocolate and leave it for 2 minutes before stirring together – it will become a gorgeous shiny smooth ganache. Pour this into the cooled pastry case and spread it out evenly.

Shake your tray of toasted hazelnuts to remove the skins (you can also use your hands, but they should easily fall off) and place the skinned nuts into a small bowl. Line a large baking tray with baking parchment ready for the next step.

To make the praline, put the sugar and 6 tablespoons of water in a medium heavy-based saucepan over a medium heat. Keep an eye on it but do not touch or stir it – after 10–15 minutes it should turn an amber colour. At this point, swirl it very gently, then tip in the hazelnuts and butter. Stir together and pour onto the lined tray. Leave to cool. Once cool, blitz half of this sugary/caramel hazelnut mix to a food processor (or smash it with a rolling pin) to create a dust. Sprinkle this dust in a circle over the tart. Break up the remaining praline into big chunks and place it at various points on the tart.

Slice and serve. Whipped cream makes for a good pairing, but is not at all necessary. Enjoy!

The tart will keep well for up to 4 days in an airtight container in the fridge without the praline topping.

Tip

Working with sugar can sound like an advanced skill, but don't let it worry you: the key to a successful caramel is to let the sugar heat for a while before stirring. If any of the sugar crystals get shocked and become cold (E.g. by touching the sides of the pan if stirred) they cause a chain reaction of crystallising, resulting in granular caramel. If this happens it isn't the end of the world because we're combining it with hazelnuts anyway! And you can fix it by adding a touch more water and keeping on the heat to break the crystals down again. I highly recommend wearing an oven glove or having a tea towel covering your hand at the final stage; hot sugar is no joke!

Peach Melba 'Eton Mess'

SERVES: 4

2 egg whites

100g (3½oz/½ cup) caster (superfine) sugar

¼ tsp white wine vinegar

Filling

350g (12oz/1¾ cups) caster (superfine) sugar

juice of ½ lemon

4 peaches

450ml (15fl oz/scant 2 cups) double (heavy) cream

300g (10½oz) raspberries

Tip

Ensure your bowl for making the meringue mixture is as clean as possible: glass or metal bowls work best. When separating whites, I avoid doing them over the same bowl, in case of any breakage (that would spoil the whites already in the bowl). Use any separating method that works for you, but I find classic shell-to-shell works best for me.

Peaches and raspberries get stacked up with meringue and cream in this fruity dessert. Built up in glasses, these make a nice change from the classic 'mess'. Use store-bought meringues for a totally no-bake, easy dessert.

Preheat the oven to 100°C fan (110°C/200°F/Gas ¼) and line a large baking tray with baking parchment (or a silicone liner).

Make the meringue by whisking the egg whites in a clean bowl with an electric handheld whisk (or in the bowl of a stand mixer fitted with the whisk attachment) on high speed until soft peaks form. Add the sugar, a tablespoon at a time, until fully incorporated, whisking continuously, then add the vinegar and keep mixing on high speed until stiff peaks form (feel free to try the 'bowl upside down over your head' trick – the meringue should not slip or move around in the bowl). If using a stand mixer, use a metal spoon to ensure no liquid has accumulated at the bottom. Use a tablespoon to dollop the meringue mixture onto the lined tray to form lots of small blobs. Bake in the oven for 1 hour – 1 hour 10 minutes, until the meringues are stiff and cream-coloured. Leave to cool in the turned-off oven until ready to assemble.

Meanwhile, poach the peaches. Put the sugar, lemon juice and about 350ml (12fl oz/1½ cups) water in a deep saucepan and heat over a high heat for a few minutes until the sugar has dissolved. Cut the peaches in half and remove the stone. Place them into the sugary water and cook for about 3 minutes, then flip to make sure the peaches are fully cooked through. Cook for another 3 minutes, and, once soft, remove and leave to drain/cool on a wire rack. Once cool, remove the skins from the peaches and slice into wedges.

Whisk the cream in a bowl with an electric handheld whisk until it forms soft peaks.

In a small bowl, smash up most of the raspberries to make a rustic puree (save a few to finish the dish). Assemble the dessert when you're ready to eat, starting with cream, then some peaches and smashed raspberries, then meringue and repeat! Finish with whole raspberries and serve!

Plum, Raspberry & Almond Tart

SERVES: 10

Shortcrust pastry

320g (11¼oz) store-bought shortcrust pastry (or see page 52 if you want to make your own)

Frangipane

120g (4¼oz) butter, softened

120g (4¼oz/⅔ cup) granulated sugar

2 medium eggs

1 tsp almond extract

120g (4¼oz/1 cup) ground almonds

Topping

4 large plums, stoned and cut into wedges

100g (3½oz) raspberries

icing (powdered) sugar, for dusting

This autumnal shortcrust pastry tart filled with an almond frangipane and topped with plums and raspberries makes for a pretty stunning display for guests.

Preheat the oven to 180°C fan (200°C/400°F/Gas 6) and lightly grease a 23cm (9in) tart tin with butter.

Unwrap the pastry and roll it out on a floured surface to a thickness of 5mm (¼in), until it's large enough to fit the tart tin. Press it into the tin, letting the pastry come up the sides and overhang the edges. Line the pastry with a sheet of baking parchment – enough to go up the sides – fill it with baking beans or raw rice so that the base is entirely covered and weighed down, then bake in the oven for 15 minutes. Remove from the oven, carefully remove the paper and beans/rice and leave to cool on a wire rack (leave the oven on).

While the pastry case is cooling, make the frangipane filling. Beat the butter and sugar with an electric mixer (or by hand with a wooden spoon for 10 minutes) until light and fluffy, then beat in the eggs and almond extract and fold in the ground almonds. Spread into the tart case. Arrange the plums in a pattern on top of the tart, along with the raspberries. Bake in the oven for 20 minutes, until golden. Let cool, dust with icing (powdered) sugar and serve with fresh cream!

The tart will keep well for up to 3 days in an airtight container.

Why not try

1. Apricot with pecans on top

2. Pear and fig

3. Christmas: dried mixed fruit combined with brandy

Chocolate & Caramel Self-saucing Pudding

SERVES: 4–6

145g (5oz/generous 1 cup) plain (all-purpose) flour

1 tsp baking powder

110g (3¾oz/½cup) granulated sugar

25g (1oz) cocoa powder

65g (2¼oz) butter, melted, plus extra for greasing

145ml (5fl oz/⅔ cup) milk

1 medium egg

100g (3½oz) caramel sauce (from a tin/jar)

150g (5½oz) milk chocolate (in bar form)

Topping

100g (3½oz/½ cup) granulated sugar

25g (1oz) cocoa powder

275ml (9¼ fl oz/generous 1 cup) boiling water

Self-saucing pudding is a fancy name for a dessert that is baked all-in-one, and the end result produces a sauce at the bottom of the dish. Scoop this warm chocolate, caramelly dessert straight into bowls and serve with a choice of cream or ice cream!

Preheat the oven to 170°C fan (190°C/370°F/Gas 5) and lightly grease a 20cm (8in) square brownie/baking tin with a little butter.

Combine the flour, baking powder, sugar and cocoa powder in a large bowl. Make a well in the dry mixture and add the melted butter, milk and egg. Whisk to form a thick batter.

In the brownie/baking tin, spread the caramel sauce over the bottom, then lay the chocolate in strips over the top. Pour the batter over this chocolate layer.

To make the topping, combine the granulated sugar and cocoa powder in a small bowl then sprinkle this over the cake mixture. Pour the boiling water over the batter evenly (I pour it onto the back of a large wooden spoon to help distribute it more evenly/with less pressure), then bake in the oven for 25–35 minutes, until the top is firm. Serve immediately, with ice cream or cream and extra caramel sauce.

Tip

Pouring the water onto the batter directly from the kettle can result in the water 'cutting through' the cake batter, making it mix together – this results in a thin batter, funny texture and no sauce. By pouring over the back of a large spoon, the water pressure reduces, meaning it sits on top of the batter instead of pushing through it.

Blackberry Meringue Pie

SERVES: 8

175g (6oz) digestive biscuits (or graham crackers)

125g (4½oz) unsalted butter, melted

50g (1¾oz/4 tbsp) granulated sugar

Filling

4 large eggs, beaten

225g (8oz) blackberries (fresh or frozen)

220g (7¾ oz/2½ cups) granulated sugar

35g (1¾oz) plain flour

zest and juice of 1 lemon

Meringue

3 egg whites

150g (5½oz) granulated sugar

A twist on the standard (whilst obviously delicious) lemon version. This makes the most of autumnal produce for something with a little extra flair! It looks fabulous with bold pink and purple colours from the fruit and covered with lashings of toasted meringue topping. To keep it extra easy, I replace the pastry base with a biscuit base.

Preheat the oven to 180°C fan (200°C/400°F/Gas 6).

Crush the biscuits until they resemble fine sand; do this either by placing them into a large sandwich bag and bashing them with a rolling pin, or simply drop them into a food processor! Once crumbly, put them in a bowl and add the melted butter and sugar. Grease a 23cm (9in) loose-bottomed tart tin or loose-bottomed cake tin with butter or baking spray and press the mixture evenly into this, pressing up the sides to create a sort of 'pastry case'. Bake for 8 minutes.

Make the filling by combining all the ingredients in a large mixing bowl or the bowl of a stand mixer. It should come together quickly. If using frozen berries, defrost them first in the microwave so you can mash them into a liquid or paste.

Pour this filling over the baked crust and return to the oven for 25–30 minutes, until no longer wobbly. Set aside whilst making the meringue.

Place the egg whites in a clean bowl and beat with a handheld electric mixer. Once soft peaks begin to form, start adding the sugar a tablespoon at a time until fully incorporated. If using a food processor have it on high for several minutes before adding the sugar.

Spread this meringue into a little mountain over the tart and blast with a blowtorch to create the toasted look, or place under a preheated grill for 5 minutes!

Black Forest Crumble

SERVES: 6

700g (1lb 9oz) pitted cherries, chopped (fresh or frozen)

75g (2½oz/⅓ cup) granulated sugar

2 tbsp lemon juice

25ml kirsch (or similar cherry liqueur)

100g (3½oz) dark chocolate, coarsely chopped

Topping

120g (4¼oz/scant 1 cup) plain (all-purpose) flour

20g (¾oz) cocoa powder

120g (4¼oz/generous 1 cup) rolled oats

100g (3½oz/½ cup) soft light brown sugar

90g (3¼oz) butter, softened

This cherry-laden crumble gives the retro flavour combination of cherries, chocolate, cream and kirsch a rude awakening. Fresh or frozen cherries are absolutely fine! With chocolate running through the filling and topping, this works really well with a good heap of thick cream.

Preheat the oven to 180°C fan (200°C/400°F/Gas 6).

Toss together the chopped cherries, sugar, lemon juice, liqueur and chocolate in a bowl. Transfer this mixture into a 23cm (9in) pie dish (or any dish at least 5cm/2in deep).

In another bowl, combine the crumble topping ingredients, using a fork to work everything together and create a wet-sand like consistency. Sprinkle this over the cherry mixture and bake in the oven for 35–40 minutes until the topping is golden and the filling bubbling around the edges.

Remove from the oven and serve warm with fresh cream or ice cream!

Why not try

1. Substitute the cherries for a berries and cherries frozen mix for something quick and easy

2. Apple and pear with dark chocolate

3. Rhubarb with white chocolate

CHILL TIME: 1 HR

BAKE TIME: 20 MINS

TOTAL: 1 HR 45 MINS

Orange & Mango Tropical Trifle

SERVES: 8

Sponge cake (or use a 300g/10½oz pound cake)

120g (4¼oz) butter, at room temperature

120g (4¼oz/⅔ cup) granulated sugar

2 medium eggs

120g (4¼oz/scant 1 cup) plain (all-purpose) flour

1 tsp baking powder

grated zest and juice of 1 lemon

Other layers

1 x 85g (3oz) packet orange jelly crystals

3 ripe mangoes, peeled, de-stoned and sliced (or 1 ripe mango and about 200g/7oz mango pulp)

500ml (17fl oz/generous 2 cups) packet fresh custard

400ml (14fl oz/1⅔ cups) double (heavy) cream

1 tbsp coconut extract

coconut flakes, to decorate (optional)

lime zest, to decorate (optional)

Layers of orange jelly, coconut cream and fresh fruit give us this tropical-themed trifle. I know lots of families have their special trifle go-to, but this is definitely worth a summertime feature! This includes a simple all-in-one cake recipe, but lady fingers will work too!

First, make the cake (if you're making your own). Preheat the oven to 180°C fan (200°C/400°F/Gas 6) and line a 20cm (8in) square brownie/baking tin with baking parchment.

In a large bowl, or the bowl of a stand mixer fitted with the beater attachment, add all the cake ingredients and combine until smooth. If very stiff, add a little milk. Pour into the lined tin, level it out, and bake in the oven for 20 minutes, until golden and a skewer inserted into the middle comes out clean. Remove from the oven and leave to cool on a wire rack.

Make the jelly according to the packet instructions and leave to set in a wide, shallow baking dish (while the cake is cooling).

Once the cake has cooled, slice it up and use it to cover the base of your trifle bowl (use any deep, glass bowl). Top with slices from 1 mango and spread the jelly over the top (it doesn't need to be neat as it'll be covered). Let set in the fridge for at least 1 hour. If you can't find mango pulp, make it using two mangoes: chop and place in a blender/use a hand blender to create a thick pulp. Spread this over the jelly. Top the jelly with the custard.

Finally, whisk the cream with the coconut extract until whipped and fluffy. Spread this over the top of the trifle and top with coconut flakes and lime zest if you have any! Serve.

15 mins **HANDS-ON TIME**

CHILL TIME: 30 MINS

BAKE TIME: 12–15 MINS

TOTAL: 57 MINS–1 HR

Make-ahead Choc-chip Cookie Ice Cream Sandwiches

MAKES: 6 ICE CREAM SANDWICHES

125g (4½oz) butter, melted

120g (4¼oz/⅔ cup) soft light brown sugar

100g (3½oz/½ cup) granulated sugar

1 medium egg

2 tsp vanilla extract

260g (9½oz/1⅔ cups) plain (all-purpose) flour

3 tsp baking powder

1 tbsp cocoa powder

200g (7oz) milk chocolate, coarsely chopped

vanilla ice cream, to serve

Make a batch of chocolate cookie dough ahead of time, freeze it as a log, then this log will be waiting for you to cut slices off and bake, before filling with ice cream. This is great for late-night snacking without a whole lot of effort. Of course, you can also make them in one go! The cookies need to cool a bit before filling with ice cream. As it lasts a while, doubling up the cookie dough to keep in the freezer is highly recommended.

In a large bowl using an electric mixer, or a stand mixer fitted with the beater attachment, combine the butter and both sugars on medium speed for several minutes, until fully combined. Add the egg and vanilla and mix again. Combine the flour, baking powder, cocoa powder and milk chocolate then fold into the wet ingredients until combined. Form the dough into a log shape on cling film (plastic wrap), wrap it up really tight and chill in the fridge for at least 30 minutes (it will keep well in the fridge for up to 4 days), or in the freezer for up to 2 months.

When ready to bake, preheat the oven to 180°C fan (200°C/400°F/Gas 6) and line two or three large baking trays with baking parchment (or silicone liners).

Slice off twelve 2cm (¾in)-thick discs of dough from the log – remember to do this in pairs as we want sandwiches at the end – and place them spaced apart on the lined baking trays. Bake in the oven for about 12 minutes, until crisp at the edges. (If you're baking them from frozen, they'll need 15 minutes.)

Remove from the oven and leave to cool before filling with ice cream and sandwiching together!

Sticky Figgy Toffee Pudding

SERVES: 6

mild cooking oil spray or butter, for greasing

180g (6½oz) dried figs, coarsely chopped

180ml (6fl oz/¾ cup) boiling water

1 tsp bicarbonate of soda (baking soda)

1 tbsp black treacle (molasses)

90g (3¼oz) butter, at room temperature

90g (3¼oz/scant ½ cup) soft dark brown sugar

90g (3¼oz/scant ½ cup) soft light brown sugar

3 medium eggs

180g (6½oz/scant 1⅓ cups) plain (all-purpose) flour

1 tsp ground ginger

1 tsp ground cardamom

1 tsp baking powder

Toffee sauce

50g (1¾oz) butter

150g (5½oz/¾ cup) soft light brown sugar

150ml (5fl oz/⅔ cup) double (heavy) cream

A British classic, with a dried fig twist, served warm with lashings of extra toffee sauce – this pudding is a gem. For those who prefer their pudding to be fruit-free, I suggest keeping the figs but blending them with a stick blender to a puree. She might not be the most attractive bake on this list, but it's all about the personality here. Ice cream, cream or custard can be served alongside – asking which your guests prefer is bound to spark dinner-table conflict...

Preheat the oven to 160°C fan (180°C/350°F/Gas 4) and grease a 23cm (9in) square baking dish with oil or butter.

Put the chopped figs, boiling water and bicarbonate of soda (baking soda) in a small saucepan and heat over a low heat for about 10 minutes, then stir in the treacle (molasses). Mash everything together using the spoon, or use a stick blender if preferred, and set aside.

In a large bowl, or the bowl of a stand mixer fitted with the beater attachment, combine the butter and both sugars until fluffy. Add the eggs one at a time, mixing after each addition, then add the fig mixture and combine again. Combine the flour, baking powder and spices then fold them in. Pour the mixture into the greased dish and bake in the oven for about 25 minutes, until a skewer inserted into the middle comes out clean.

Make the sauce while the pudding is in the oven by combining the butter, sugar and cream in a saucepan over a low heat until combined, then turn up the heat so it bubbles for 3–4 minutes. Turn off the heat and pour most of it onto the just-baked sponge. Slice and serve while warm, adding any remaining toffee sauce and your choice of creamy topping!

The pudding will keep well for up to 4 days in an airtight container in the fridge.

15 mins HANDS-ON TIME

REST TIME: 15 MINS

BAKE TIME: 30 MINS

TOTAL: 1 HR

Leftover Almond Croissant Bread & Butter Pudding

SERVES: 6

8 almond croissants

4 medium eggs

2½ tbsp granulated sugar

380ml (13fl oz/1⅔ cups) double (heavy) cream

220ml (7½fl oz/scant 1 cup) milk

50ml (1¾fl oz/3½ tbsp) Amaretto (almond liqueur)

This is sort of referring back to those almond croissants on page 18, but if I'm being totally honest I don't know who has leftover croissants ... Bread & butter pudding is a great way to use up slightly stale carbs, and I think almond croissants make a far more exciting pudding than your standard white bread!

Preheat the oven to 160°C fan (180°C/350°F/Gas 4).

Slice the almond croissants in half lengthways and place them in a buttered ovenproof baking dish, about 20 x 30cm (8 x 12in).

Whisk together the eggs and sugar in a large bowl and set aside.

Heat the cream and milk in a saucepan until simmering and just about boiling. Whisk it into the egg/sugar mix then add the Amaretto. Pour this over the croissants and let them rest about 15 minutes while the oven gets hot.

Once hot, bake the pudding for about 30 minutes until golden and the tops of the croissants are getting toasty! Serve warm.

Espresso Martini Cake

SERVES: 8

175g (6oz/scant 1¼ cups) plain (all-purpose) flour

1 tsp baking powder

1 tsp bicarbonate of soda (baking soda)

2 tbsp cocoa powder

160g (5½oz/¾ cup) granulated sugar

pinch of fine sea salt

100ml (3½fl oz/scant ½ cup) boiling water

2 tsp unsweetened hot chocolate powder

2 tsp instant coffee powder/ granules

60ml (2fl oz/¼ cup) milk

2 medium eggs

2 tbsp golden syrup (corn syrup)

2 tbsp vegetable oil

Buttercream frosting

120g (4¼oz) butter, at room temperature

275g (9¾oz/2½ cups) icing (powdered) sugar

2 tbsp coffee liqueur (or half a shot of espresso, or 2 tsp instant coffee mixed into 2 tbsp water)

coffee beans or cocoa powder, to decorate

A single-layer fudgy chocolate and coffee cake topped with a thick, coffee liqueur-laden frosting (as always, alcohol is optional with notes for substitutes). 'Spressy Marts', as my partner calls them, are the first cocktail we learned to make during lockdown. I think I realistically prefer the cake to the cocktail, but either way, this is a killer way to end an evening.

Preheat the oven to 160°C fan (180°C/350°F/Gas 4) and line a 20cm (8in) round cake tin with baking parchment.

In a large bowl, or the bowl of a stand mixer fitted with the beater attachment, combine the flour, baking powder, bicarbonate of soda (baking soda), cocoa powder, sugar and salt.

Combine the boiling water, hot chocolate powder, instant coffee and milk in a mug. Set aside.

Make a well in the dry mixture, add the eggs, syrup and oil, and mix to thoroughly combine, then slowly pour in the hot chocolate mixture until it has all been incorporated. The batter will be fairly thin. Pour the batter into the lined tin and bake in the oven for 30–40 minutes, until a skewer inserted into the middle comes out clean.

Remove from the oven and leave to cool in the tin on a wire rack.

Once cool, make the buttercream. Beat the butter on high speed with an electric mixer until soft, then add half the icing (powdered) sugar and mix for several minutes until combined. Add the remaining icing sugar and the coffee liqueur or substitute until the buttercream is spreadable. Spread over the cake, top with a dusting of cocoa powder or some coffee beans to decorate, then serve!

The cake will keep for up to 3 days in an airtight container in the fridge.

30 mins **HANDS-ON TIME**

BAKE TIME: 42 MINS

CHILL TIME: 2 HRS

TOTAL: 3 HRS 12 MINS

Apple Pie Cheesecake Bars

MAKES: 16 SMALL BARS

Cheesecake layer

150g (5½oz) Granny Smith apples, peeled and diced

2 tsp ground cinnamon

2 tbsp soft light brown sugar

150g (5½oz) white chocolate, chopped

400g (14oz) full-fat cream cheese

50g (1¾oz/4 tbsp) granulated sugar

1 tbsp plain (all-purpose) flour

1 tsp vanilla extract

1 tsp lemon juice

2 medium eggs

Base

250g (9oz) digestive biscuits (or graham crackers)

100g (3½oz) butter, melted

Stewed cinnamon apples run throughout the cheesecake layer of these bars. They are just like a baked cheesecake, but are made in a square tin (tray) and cut into squares for easy snackable bites! This recipe is a great way to use up any gluts of apples you may have.

Preheat the oven to 180°C fan (200°C/400°F/Gas 6) and line a 20cm (8in) square brownie/baking tin with baking parchment.

Put the apples, cinnamon and brown sugar in a saucepan and cook over a medium heat for 5–10 minutes until softened and caramelised. Drain off any excess liquid and set aside.

Melt the white chocolate in the microwave in 15-second intervals, stirring regularly, until smooth. Set aside to cool.

Smash up the biscuits in a bowl (or use a food processor) until they reach a fine crumb. Stir in the melted butter and press the mixture into the lined baking tin. Ensure the biscuit level is even, then bake in the oven for 7 minutes. Once baked, cool on a wire rack and keep the oven on.

Make the cheesecake mixture by whisking the cream cheese in a large bowl with an electric handheld whisk (or stand mixer) on high speed for about 2 minutes, then add the sugar and whisk for another 2 minutes. Add the flour, vanilla extract, lemon juice and eggs and combine again, then add the melted (and cooled) white chocolate. Fold together with a spatula or wooden spoon, until just combined. Pour half of the cheesecake mixture over the baked base, then spoon about half of the apple mixture over the cheesecake.

Pour over the remaining cheesecake mixture. Again, spoon the rest of the apple mixture over the cheesecake and top with the apple cooking liquid. Swirl using a spoon. Bake in the oven for 35 minutes, until the edges are golden and the middle looks just set.

Leave to cool on a wire rack until room temperature, then chill in the fridge for at least 2 hours before slicing into 16 bars and serving!

The bars will keep well in the fridge for up to 4–5 days in an airtight container.

late-night treats

Blackberry & White Chocolate Cheesecake Brownies

MAKES: 9 BROWNIES

100g (3½oz) dark chocolate, chopped

170g (5¾oz) butter, melted

100g (3½oz/½ cup) granulated sugar

100g (3½oz/½ cup) soft light brown sugar

2 medium eggs

85g (3oz/generous ½ cup) plain (all-purpose) flour

30g (1oz) cocoa powder

150g (5½oz) white chocolate, coarsely chopped

75g (2½oz) blackberries, coarsely chopped

Cheesecake topping

120g (4¼oz) full-fat cream cheese

1 medium egg

50g (1¾oz/4 tbsp) granulated sugar

75g (2½oz) blackberries

Blackberry, white chocolate and cheesecake all intertwined in a brownie. Cheesecake-layered brownies are usually my most viewed social media posts and website recipes, and this makes a great twist. They're totally unnecessary, but an absolute delight, and I think the blackberries cut through all the richness for a really well-balanced bake.

Preheat the oven to 180°C fan (200°C/400°F/Gas 6) and line a 20cm (8in) square brownie/baking tin with baking parchment.

Melt the dark chocolate in the microwave in 20-second intervals, stirring regularly to make sure it doesn't burn. Set aside to cool while making the brownie batter.

In a large mixing bowl, with an electric handheld whisk, or in the bowl of a stand mixer fitted with the whisk attachment, whisk together the melted butter and both sugars for 3–5 minutes until totally combined. Add the eggs, one at a time, mixing after each addition. Check the melted chocolate has cooled a little, and then gradually add it and mix to combine. Add the flour, cocoa powder, chopped white chocolate and blackberries and fold together. Transfer the batter into the lined tin.

Make the cheesecake layer by combining all ingredients in a small bowl and mixing with a spoon. Pour this over the brownies. Roughly fold together with a teaspoon and scatter over the remaining blackberries.

Bake in the oven for 20–30 minutes, until the cheesecake layer looks a little golden. The cheesecake may look a little wobbly but that's fine; it sets as it cools.

Remove from the oven and leave to cool in the tin on a wire rack before slicing and serving!

The brownies will keep for up to 4 days in an airtight container.

Molten Salted Caramel Brownie Skillet

SERVES: 4–6

Salted caramel

150g (5½oz/¾ cup) granulated sugar

70g (2½oz) butter

90ml (3fl oz/6 tbsp) double (heavy) cream

1 tsp sea salt flakes

Brownie

100g (3½oz) dark chocolate, chopped

170g (5¾oz) butter, melted, plus extra for greasing

100g (3½oz/½ cup) soft light brown sugar

100g (3½oz/½ cup) granulated sugar

2 medium eggs

2 tsp vanilla extract

85g (3oz/generous ½ cup) plain (all-purpose) flour

30g (1oz) cocoa powder

100g (3½oz) milk chocolate, coarsely chopped

100g (3½oz) soft caramels or caramel chocolates, coarsely chopped

vanilla ice cream, to serve

Puddles of salted caramel run throughout this brownie skillet. Fudgy, decadent and just right when you need real comfort, this is one to eat warm, topping it with lots of vanilla or caramel ice cream. The homemade salted caramel is what really elevates this and is easier to make than you might think!

Start by making the salted caramel. Put the sugar and 1 tablespoon of water in a saucepan over a medium heat. Stir it a little with a wooden spoon but avoid letting the sugar climb up the side of the pan. It might look clumpy and crystallised but stick with it. Once the sugar has turned amber in colour and is all melted, add the butter in one go and stir rapidly. It will froth a bit, so take care with this step! Cook for 1 minute, then stir in the cream and cook for a further minute. Remove from heat, add the salt flakes and set aside.

Preheat the oven to 180°C fan (200°C/400°F/Gas 6) and grease a 20cm (8in) skillet or cake tin with butter.

Melt the dark chocolate in the microwave in 20-second intervals, stirring regularly to make sure it doesn't burn.

In a large mixing bowl, with an electric handheld whisk, or in the bowl of a stand mixer fitted with the whisk attachment, whisk the melted butter and both sugars for 3–5 minutes until totally combined. Add the eggs, one at a time, mixing after each addition, then add the vanilla extract and mix again. Gradually add the cooled melted chocolate and mix to combine. Fold in the flour, cocoa powder and chopped chocolate and caramels into the wet mixture with a rubber spatula or wooden spoon until just combined.

Transfer the batter into the skillet and bake in the oven for 25–27 minutes, until golden on top and with only the slightest wobble in the middle. Drizzle over the salted caramel, top with ice cream and serve immediately!

If you like, you can store the leftovers like brownies, slicing them and keeping them in an airtight container for up to 4–5 days.

Tip

If you don't have a cast-iron/ovenproof skillet, use a cake pan and follow the same steps. A shallow pan is absolutely fine as the batter doesn't puff up too much. When making the caramel, if it continues to look too crystalline, add a little water and turn down the heat, letting the crystals melt.

Peanut Butter & Jelly Blondies

MAKES: 9 BLONDIES

125g (4½oz) white chocolate, chopped

170g (5¾oz) butter, melted

4 tbsp peanut butter

75g (2½oz/⅓ cups) soft light brown sugar

125g (4½oz/generous ½ cup) granulated sugar

2 medium eggs

1 tbsp golden syrup (corn syrup) or honey or other sticky syrup

2 tsp vanilla extract

110g (3¾oz/generous ⅔ cup) plain (all-purpose) flour

100g (3½oz) raspberries

100g (3½oz) salted peanuts

4 tbsp raspberry jam

A classic American combo, turned into a fudgy blondie recipe. These have a similar richness to brownies but are made with white chocolate instead. Any peanut butter will work here and feel free to use the flavoured jam/jelly/ preserve that you like!

Preheat the oven to 180°C fan (200°C/400°F/Gas 6) and line a 20cm (8in) square brownie/baking tin with baking parchment.

Melt the white chocolate in the microwave in 20-second intervals, stirring regularly to make sure it doesn't burn. Set aside to cool while making the brownie batter.

In a large mixing bowl, with an electric handheld whisk, or in the bowl of a stand mixer fitted with the whisk attachment, whisk together the melted butter, 1 tablespoon of the peanut butter and both sugars for 3–5 minutes until totally combined. Add the eggs, syrup or honey and vanilla extract and mix again, then whisk in the cooled melted white chocolate until fully incorporated. Fold in the flour, raspberries and peanuts and transfer to the lined tin. Dollop on and swirl with a knife the remaining 3 tablespoons of peanut butter and all the jam over the blondie batter.

Bake in the oven for 30 minutes, until golden on top and with only the slightest wobble in the middle. Remove from the oven and leave to cool in the tin on a wire rack before slicing and serving.

The blondies will keep for up to 4 days in an airtight container.

Why not try

1. Almond butter with blueberry jam

2. Cashew butter with marmalade

3. Cocoa peanut butter with strawberry jam

FREEZE TIME: 45 MINS

BAKE TIME: 30 MINS

TOTAL: 1 HR 35 MINS

Nutella Layered Brownies

MAKES: 9 BROWNIES

200g (7oz) Nutella or other chocolate hazelnut spread

100g (3½oz) dark chocolate, chopped

170g (5¾oz) butter, melted

100g (3½oz/½ cup) granulated sugar

100g (3½oz/½ cup) soft light brown sugar

2 medium eggs

1 tsp vanilla extract

85g (3oz/generous ½ cup) plain (all-purpose) flour

30g (1oz) cocoa powder

small pinch of fine sea salt

This is the result of needing something on some of my darker days, those days when getting out of bed can feel a little harder or perhaps it's just a day that requires unthinkable amounts of chocolate. The Nutella gets frozen in a layer that then goes in the middle of the brownie batter for a delicious melty middle!

Line a 20cm (8in) square brownie/baking tin with baking parchment.

Loosen the Nutella in a bowl in the microwave for 30 seconds, then spread it over the base of the lined brownie/baking tin to form an even layer. Place in the freezer for 45 minutes. Once frozen into a solid layer, remove the baking parchment and Nutella from the tin and freeze the parchment and Nutella again.

Preheat the oven to 180°C fan (200°C/400°F/Gas 6) and line that same brownie/baking tin with more baking parchment.

Melt the dark chocolate in the microwave in 20-second intervals, stirring regularly to make sure it doesn't burn. Set aside.

In a large mixing bowl, with an electric handheld whisk, or in the bowl of a stand mixer fitted with the whisk attachment, whisk together the melted butter and both sugars for 3–5 minutes until totally combined. Add the eggs and vanilla extract and mix again. Gradually add the cooled melted chocolate and mix to combine. Add the flour, cocoa powder and salt and fold gently to combine.

Transfer half the batter into the lined tin, then top with the layer of frozen Nutella, before pouring over the remaining batter. Bake in the oven for 30 minutes, until golden on top and with only the slightest wobble in the middle.

Remove from the oven and leave to cool in the tin on a wire rack before slicing to make 9 brownies.

The brownies will keep for up to 5 days in an airtight container.

Key Lime Pie Shortbread Cookies

MAKES: 15 COOKIES

100g (3½oz) butter, at room temperature

50g (1¾oz/4 tbsp) granulated sugar

175g (6oz/scant 1¼ cups) plain (all-purpose) flour, plus extra for dusting

1 tbsp grated lime zest, plus a little extra to serve

pinch of fine sea salt

Glaze

150g (5½oz/1¼ cups) icing (powdered) sugar

1½ tbsp lime juice

There's just something about the flavour and smell of lime that I love. This recipe takes classic lime flavours and transforms them into cute cookies. I recommend making these for summery events – they are perfectly light and crisp. They also keep/travel well once the glaze has set.

Preheat the oven to 130°C fan (150°C/300°F/Gas 2) and line two large baking trays with baking parchment.

Beat the butter in a large bowl for several minutes to soften – this is easiest with a stand mixer or electric handheld whisk. Add the sugar and continue to beat until fully incorporated, then add the flour, lime zest and salt and beat again until the mixture comes together: it should hold together as a solid dough when you press it with your hands.

Roll out the dough onto a lightly floured surface to a thickness of 1–2cm (½–¾in), then cut out about 15 rounds with a small round cookie cutter (about 6cm/2 ½in) and place on the lined trays – they don't need to be too spaced out as they won't spread. Bake in the oven for 15–20 minutes, until only just turning golden at the edges. Remove from the oven, transfer to a wire rack and leave to cool.

Once the cookies are cool, make the glaze by combining the icing (powdered) sugar and lime juice. It should be very thick, only just spreadable. Spread about half a teaspoon of the glaze over each cookie, grate over more lime zest and leave to set on a wire rack for about 20 minutes before eating.

The cookies will keep well for up to 5 days in an airtight container.

Cherry Florentine Hearts

MAKES: ABOUT 15 HEARTS

60g (2¼oz) butter

60g (2¼oz) golden syrup (corn syrup) or light molasses

60g (2¼oz/¼ cup) soft light brown sugar

60g (2¼oz/scant ½ cup) plain (all-purpose) flour

65g (2¼oz) glacé cherries, finely chopped

65g (2¼oz) flaked (slivered) almonds, finely chopped

30g (1oz) mixed peel

grated zest of 1 orange

200g (7oz) dark chocolate, chopped

These chewy, chocolate-y, cherry cookies are a terrific Valentine's bake, and make for a really cute gift. Florentines have it all – nuts, dried fruit and lots of chocolate – and these are a slightly more glamorous heart-shaped version of the classic. You will need a heart-shaped cookie cutter ideally – I find shaping them freehand with a spoon can result in them being a little 'splodgy' looking.

Preheat the oven to 160°C fan (180°C/350°F/Gas 4) and line two large baking trays with baking parchment (or a silicone liner).

Put the butter, syrup and sugar in a small saucepan and heat gently until melted together, then turn off the heat and whisk in the flour. Add the cherries, almonds, mixed peel and a little of the orange zest and stir together.

Place your heart-shaped cookie cutter (mine are about 5cm/2in wide at the widest point) onto one of the baking trays and spoon about a tablespoon of the mixture into this. Leave space for spreading and repeat with the rest of the mixture. Bake in the oven for 10 minutes until golden.

Remove from the oven and leave to cool on a wire rack.

Melt the dark chocolate in the microwave in 20-second intervals, stirring regularly to make sure it doesn't burn. Once melted, spread the chocolate over the base of each of the cooled cookies. Once cooled a little, use a fork to draw 'waves' on the chocolate. Add the rest of the orange zest to the chocolate and leave to set before eating.

The hearts will keep for up to 5 days in an airtight container.

HANDS-ON TIME

CHILL TIME: 30 MINS

BAKE TIME: 30 MINS

TOTAL: 1 HR 10 MINS

Chocolate Chunk Shortbread

MAKES: 4 LARGE SHORTBREAD SQUARES

120g (4¼oz) cold butter, cubed

100g (3½oz/½ cup) granulated sugar, plus extra for sprinkling

200g (7oz/1½ cups) plain (all-purpose) flour

100g (3½oz) milk chocolate, coarsely chopped

50g (1¾oz) dark chocolate, coarsely chopped

These are just like those that you get in the bakery, but cheaper and so much better! This recipe will make sure that you nail that crisp/crumbly balance to perfection. I recommend making the shortbread in a food processor if you have one, otherwise any electric mixer will work. I use both milk and dark chocolate for the best combo, but use any blend of chocolates that you like. Feel free to double up the recipe and bake in batches or, if you have two 20cm (8in) tins, simply bake, them at the same time.

In a large bowl, or in a food processor, beat the butter and 75g (2½oz) of the sugar on high speed until fully combined, then add the flour and mix again on high speed until the mixture resembles breadcrumbs. At this stage, you should be able to 'squeeze' the mixture into a dough. Form the dough into a ball, wrap it in cling film (plastic wrap) and chill in the fridge for 30 minutes.

Preheat the oven to 150°C fan (170°C/340°F/Gas 3) and line a 20cm (8in) square brownie/baking tin with baking parchment.

Remove the dough from the fridge, unwrap it and put it directly into the lined tin. Add the chopped chocolate and press the dough and chocolate to the edges, ensuring the shortbread is spread evenly – it will be crumbly. Sprinkle over the remaining 25g (1oz) of granulated sugar and use a sharp knife to cut the shortbread into quarters. Bake in the oven for about 30 minutes, until the top is golden.

Remove from the oven and leave to cool before removing from the tin. You may need to run a knife over the lines again to ensure clean edges. Sprinkle over a little extra sugar, if you want, before serving.

The shortbread will keep for up to 5 days in an airtight container.

HANDS-ON TIME

TOTAL: 10 MINS

Chocolate Orange Ice Cream Sundae

SERVES: 2

150g (5½oz) orange chocolate, broken into chunks

4 tbsp orange marmalade

4 scoops vanilla ice cream

4 scoops chocolate ice cream

2 shortbread biscuits

optional extras: leftover brownies (such as my Ultimate Chocolate Brownies on page 24), chocolate orange biscuits

This dessert is really quick to whip up, then you can let everyone decorate it as they wish. It's less of a recipe, more of an assembly job, but that definitely doesn't take away from the fact you'll have made something delicious! I know orange chocolate can sometimes be a bit controversial, but I think it's a genuine pleasure in life. Especially when one of those Terry's Chocolate Oranges is involved and you get to smash it against the wall...

Melt all but two chunks (to decorate) of the orange chocolate in the microwave in 20-second intervals, stirring regularly to prevent burning.

In tall glasses, layer up marmalade, followed by a scoop of ice cream, a drizzle of the melted chocolate, then more marmalade, and more ice cream on top. Top with shortbread and drizzle the last of the chocolate sauce on top. Add the remaining chunks of chocolate and serve.

Why not try

1. Banoffee – replacing the marmalade with caramel sauce and adding bananas

2. Boozy hot fudge brownie – add layers of brownie and pour over Irish cream liqueur!

3. DIY ice-cream sundae bar – set up a station with various toppings and sauces, letting everyone build their own!

Funfetti Frosted Cookies

MAKES: 12 COOKIES

125g (4½oz) butter, melted

120g (4¼oz/⅔ cup) soft light brown sugar

100g (3½oz/½ cup) granulated sugar

1 medium egg

2 tsp vanilla extract

275g (9¾oz/2¼ cups) plain (all-purpose) flour

3 tsp baking powder

1 tbsp multi-coloured sprinkles

Buttercream frosting

100g (3½oz) butter, at room temperature

1 tsp vanilla extract

300g (10½oz/2¾ cups) icing (powdered) sugar

a little milk, if needed

pink food colouring

multi-coloured sprinkles, to decorate

Because cookies definitely need to be made MORE extra – these vanilla-heavy cookies get topped with a fluffy pink buttercream and sprinkles for fairy birthday party vibes. Go wild with the decorations, using whatever you like and opting for another colour for the buttercream if preferred. I like to use gel food colouring – it goes so much further than the little bottles, but any will work just fine.

In a large bowl using an electric handheld whisk, or in the bowl of a stand mixer fitted with the whisk attachment, whisk the butter and both sugars on medium speed for several minutes, until fully combined (if you do this with a hand whisk, you'll need to whisk it for longer). Add the egg and vanilla extract and mix again. Combine the flour, baking powder and sprinkles then fold into the wet mixture until combined. The dough should be fairly solid at this stage (it ought to almost form a ball, albeit a very soft one!). Form the dough into a ball, wrap in cling film (plastic wrap) and chill in the fridge for at least 30 minutes.

Preheat the oven to 180°C fan (200°C/400°F/Gas 6) and line two or three large baking trays with baking parchment (or silicone liners).

continued overleaf

Unwrap the chilled dough and use a tablespoon to scoop 12 pieces of dough. Roll the pieces into balls and place them on the lined baking trays. Bake in the oven for 12 minutes, until golden and just crisping up at the edges (they continue to cook a little once removed).

Remove from the oven and leave to cool on a wire rack.

To make the buttercream, put the butter and vanilla extract in a large bowl and beat with a whisk on high speed for a minute to soften. Add half the icing (powdered) sugar and whisk on high to incorporate, then add the remaining sugar and whisk on high speed until fluffy. Add more sugar or some milk as required, along with a few drops of food colouring, until it reaches your desired consistency – it needs to be spreadable – and colour. Spread it over the cooled cookies and top with sprinkles!

The cookies will keep well for up to 4 days in an airtight container in the fridge.

Why not try
DECORATION IDEAS

1. Blue frosting with underwater theme decorations

2. Baby shower-themed frosting with special decorations

3. Holiday themes like Halloween or St Patrick's Day

10 mins   **HANDS-ON TIME**

COOK TIME: 5 MINS

TOTAL: 15 MINS

Caramelised Bananas with Ice Cream, Pecans & Caramel

SERVES: 2

3 ripe bananas

3 tbsp butter

2 tbsp honey

1 tsp ground cinnamon

vanilla ice cream

handful of pecans, crushed

Ripe bananas, pan-fried in a caramel/cinnamon sauce, before being topped with ice cream and scatterings of pecans: that hot/cold situation is the epitome of late-night treat. And this can be conjured up in less than 10 minutes!

Peel the bananas and slice them at an angle into diagonal discs about 1cm (½in) thick.

Heat a frying pan (skillet) over a medium heat and add the butter, honey and cinnamon. Once the butter has melted, add the slices of banana and fry for about 2 minutes before flipping and frying for another 2 minutes. They should look golden and caramelised.

Place in a bowl, top with ice cream, a scattering of crushed pecans and the caramel sauce from the pan (or add more caramel from a bottle/jar) and serve immediately!

Boyfriend Triple Chocolate Cookies

MAKES: 12 COOKIES

110g (3¾oz) butter, softened

100g (3½oz/½ cup) soft light brown sugar

100g (3½oz/½ cup) granulated sugar

1 medium egg

1 tsp vanilla extract

160g (5½oz/generous 1 cup) plain (all-purpose) flour

30g (1oz) cocoa powder

½ tsp bicarbonate of soda (baking soda)

pinch of fine sea salt

150g (5½oz) white chocolate, coarsely chopped (or white chocolate chips)

100g (3½oz) milk chocolate, coarsely chopped (or milk chocolate chips)

These are the first thing I ever baked for my partner, and up until the Husband Tart came about (see page 112), they were his favourite thing. I baked up a batch of these in our early days of dating, left about 8 in a container on his work desk (we met through work) and crept away before he arrived for the day. The rest, as they say, is history. These cookies come together so easily – with no fridge chill required. Feel free to use your favourite chocolate, and double up the quantity if you really want to go for it!

Preheat the oven to 180°C fan (200°C/400°F/Gas 6) and line two or three large baking trays with baking parchment (or silicone liners).

In a large bowl, or the bowl of a stand mixer fitted with the beater attachment, combine the butter and both the sugars until light and fluffy, then add the egg and vanilla and mix again. Add the flour, cocoa powder, bicarbonate of soda (baking soda) and the pinch of salt and stir together until just combined. Add most of the chopped chocolate, reserving some to sprinkle on top prior to baking.

Use a tablespoon or small ice-cream scoop to scoop the mixture onto the trays – about 3 or 4 cookies per tray, as they spread a lot! The mixture should make 12 cookies in total. Press them down with wet hands, just a little, scatter the reserved chocolate over the top and bake in the oven for 15 minutes. They will continue to cook a little once out of the oven, so don't wait until they get too dark! Remove the trays and leave to cool. Repeat for remaining batter if you didn't have enough trays to bake them all at once.

The cookies will keep for up to 5 days in an airtight container.

Tip

You can also freeze the dough before baking, to be pulled out when you are ready to bake a few at a time! Open-freeze as balls of dough, then bag up and re-freeze them, ready to bake from frozen, adding 2–3 minutes to the baking time.

Vegan Cinnamon-spiced Crinkle Cookies

10 mins HANDS-ON TIME

BAKE TIME: 12 MINS

TOTAL: 22 MINS

MAKES: 8 COOKIES

220g (7¾oz/generous 1½ cups) plain (all-purpose) flour

1½ tsp baking powder

1½ tsp bicarbonate of soda (baking soda)

2 tsp ground cinnamon

1 tsp ground ginger

60g (2¼oz/¼ cup) granulated sugar

50g (1¾oz/4 tbsp) soft light brown sugar

6 tbsp golden syrup (corn syrup) or light molasses

100g (3½oz) vegan butter, melted

There's no chill time required for these autumnal spiced crinkle cookies. Packed full of cinnamon flavours and ready in less than 30 minutes, these are the one to pair with a glass of milk (or something a little more grown-up) for the perfect cosy evening.

Preheat the oven to 180°C fan (200°C/400°F/Gas 6) and line two or three large baking sheets with baking parchment (or silicone liners).

In a large bowl, combine the flour, baking powder, bicarbonate of soda (baking soda) and spices and gently mix to combine. Add both sugars and mix again, then make a well in the dry mixture.

Heat the golden syrup in the microwave for about 20 seconds, until runny. Add the melted butter and runny golden syrup or light molasses to the well in the dry ingredients and stir to form a cookie dough.

Scoop out heaped tablespoons of the dough and roll each spoonful into about 8 balls. Place them spread apart on the lined baking sheets – at least 5cm (2in) apart – and bake in the oven for 12 minutes, until golden. Remove from the oven and leave to cool on a wire rack.

The cookies will keep for up to 5 days in an airtight container.

Tip

These are a good one to make for freezing – simply open-freeze as balls of dough, then bag up and return to the freezer, ready to bake from frozen. Then, when the mood hits you, pop onto a tray and bake, adding 2–3 minutes to the bake time!

S'mores Cookie Cups

MAKES: 8 COOKIE CUPS

mild cooking oil spray

115g (4oz) butter, melted

50g (1¾oz/4 tbsp) granulated sugar

175g (6oz/generous ¾ cup) soft light brown sugar

1 medium egg

2 tsp vanilla extract

275g (9¾oz/2¼ cups) plain (all-purpose) flour

1 tsp baking powder

pinch of fine sea salt

1 tbsp cornflour (cornstarch)

150g (5½oz) milk chocolate chips

200g (7oz) milk chocolate, broken into pieces

digestive biscuits (or graham crackers), to decorate

Meringue

3 egg whites

150g (5½oz/scant 1 cup) granulated sugar

These MEGA cookie cups are an ideal dessert or late-night snack when you fancy something cookie-like, but far more glamorous. This is the sassy aunt to a regular chocolate chip cookie and brings you s'mores flavours without needing to sit outside for hours. The meringue topper gets popped under the grill or you use a blowtorch for that fireside scorch effect!

Preheat the oven to 180°C fan (200°C/400°F/Gas 6) and grease 8 holes of a 12-hole muffin tin (tray) with oil.

In a large bowl with an electric handheld whisk, or the bowl of a stand mixer fitted with the whisk attachment, whisk together the melted butter and both sugars for 3–5 minutes until totally combined. Add the egg and vanilla extract and mix again. Combine the flour, baking powder, salt and cornflour (cornstarch) then fold them gently into the wet mixture and fold in the milk chocolate chips.

Use an ice-cream scoop or your hands to form 8 evenly-sized balls of dough, then place them in the greased muffin tin holes and bake in the oven for 12–18 minutes, until golden on top. Remove from the oven and use a small jar or similar (I use an egg cup) to create indentations in the middle of each cookie cup while they're still warm.

Melt the broken milk chocolate in the microwave in 20-second intervals, stirring regularly, then spoon about 1½–2 tablespoons into each cookie cup. Leave to cool a little then transfer to the fridge to set while making the meringue.

Make the meringue by whisking the egg whites in a clean bowl with an electric handheld whisk (or in the bowl of a stand mixer fitted with the whisk attachment) on high speed until soft peaks form. Add the sugar, a tablespoon at a time, until fully incorporated, and keep mixing on high speed until stiff peaks form. If using a stand mixer, use a metal spoon to ensure no liquid has accumulated at the bottom.

Pipe or spoon the meringue over the cupcakes and grill for 3–5 minutes or torch with a kitchen blowtorch. Scatter over some crushed digestive biscuits or graham crackers. Serve!

Butterscotch & White Chocolate Cookies

MAKES: 12 COOKIES

125g (4½oz) butter, melted

120g (4¼oz/⅔ cup) soft light brown sugar

100g (3½oz/½ cup) granulated sugar

1 medium egg

2 tsp vanilla extract

240g (8½oz/scant 2 cups) plain (all-purpose) flour

3 tsp baking powder

50g (1¾oz) butterscotch pudding/Angel Delight powder

150g (5½oz) white chocolate chips

100g (3½oz) butterscotch or toffee chips

There is something about a fairly classic cookie that always entices me. This recipe does require just a little chill time, but I promise it is very worth the wait! Butterscotch pudding/ Angel Delight powder goes into the cookie dough along with white chocolate chunks for a creamy, buttery toffee flavour.

In a large bowl with an electric handheld whisk, or in the bowl of a stand mixer fitted with the beater attachment, combine the butter and both sugars on medium speed for several minutes, until fully combined. Add the egg and vanilla extract and mix again. Add all the remaining ingredients and fold until combined. The dough should be fairly solid at this stage (it ought to almost form a ball, albeit a very soft one). Wrap in cling film (plastic wrap) and chill in the fridge for at least 30 minutes.

Preheat the oven to 180°C fan (200°C/400°F/Gas 6) and line two or three large baking trays with baking parchment (or silicone liners).

Roll the dough into about 12 balls (use a tablespoon to scoop balls of dough) and place them on the lined baking trays, spaced apart to allow for spreading. Bake in the oven for 12 minutes, until golden and just crisping up at the edges (they continue to cook a little once removed). Remove from the oven and leave to cool on a wire rack.

The cookies will keep for up to 5 days in an airtight container.

Tip

You can also freeze the dough before baking, to be pulled out when you are ready just to bake a few at a time! Open-freeze as balls of dough, then bag up and return to the freezer, ready to bake from frozen, adding 2–3 minutes to the baking time.

20 mins HANDS-ON TIME

BAKE TIME: 25 MINS

TOTAL: 45 MINS

Biscoff Traybake Cake

SERVES: 9

100g (3½oz) butter, at room temperature, plus extra for greasing

2 tbsp Biscoff (cookie butter) spread

150g (5½oz/¾ cup) granulated sugar

2 medium eggs

150g (5½oz/generous 1 cup) plain (all-purpose) flour

1 tsp baking powder

pinch of fine sea salt

½ tsp bicarbonate of soda (baking soda)

2 tbsp milk

Buttercream frosting

75g (2½oz) butter, at room temperature

75g (2½oz) smooth Biscoff (cookie butter) spread

400g (14oz/generous 3 cups) icing (powdered) sugar

Biscoff biscuits, to decorate

A Biscoff lover's dream in a super-easy cake recipe, and the frosting is equally foolproof and fabulous! This makes a 20cm (8in) square cake but can be doubled for a layered celebration cake (double the frosting quantity too)! I recommend smooth Biscoff (or any cookie butter) spread for the cake and the frosting and use any variation of Biscoff biscuits you like to decorate.

Preheat the oven to 180°C fan (200°C/400°F/Gas 6) and line a 20cm (8in) square brownie/baking tin with baking parchment or grease it with butter.

In a large mixing bowl with an electric handheld whisk, or in the bowl of a stand mixer fitted with the whisk attachment, whisk together the butter, Biscoff (cookie butter) spread and sugar for 3–5 minutes until totally combined. Add the eggs and mix again. Add the flour, baking powder, a pinch of salt and the bicarbonate of soda (baking soda) and fold together with a rubber spatula or wooden spoon, then add the milk to thin the cake batter a little. Transfer the mixture to the lined or greased tin, level it out, and bake in the oven for 25 minutes, until a skewer inserted into the middle comes out clean.

Remove from the oven and leave to cool in the tin on a wire rack.

Make the buttercream by combining the butter and Biscoff (cookie butter) spread on a high speed with an electric mixer for several minutes until soft. Add half the icing (powdered) sugar and beat to combine, then continue to add more sugar until the buttercream reaches the desired consistency.

Spread the buttercream over the cake, decorate with Biscoff biscuits and serve!

The cake will keep for up to 3 days in an airtight container in the fridge (without the biscuit decoration).

Index

Acknowledgements

This book came from a place of love for baking, for spending time in the kitchen and for the solace I found in creating (and eating) delicious things. Without wanting to sound clichéd, these bakes all have a special place in my heart and always contain love as an ingredient. That said, none of this would have ever existed without some wonderful people.

To my partner, best friend, husband, chief taste-tester and biggest cheerleader, Ian – thank you. I wouldn't be able to do all of this without your unwavering support, the love of my creations, the hugs when things go disastrously wrong and all the words of wisdom for the past several years of Tasting Thyme. It can be easy to see a social media profile and only see the front, but this partnership is what allows my passion for and relationship with food to thrive. I wouldn't have got to this point with baking and food, and in life altogether, without all that you do for me.

To Mum, Dad, Emily, Grace, Isabel – your advice, laughter, honest opinions (not always asked for/wanted!) have built me to be the baker that I am. From jam puffs to profiteroles, thank you for a childhood of seeing the kitchen and food as a place of messy joy, and a way to share and be together.

To Eleanor, my publisher, thank you for taking a chance on me! And to the entire PTB team (editorial, marketing and photography), thank you for all the hard work that brought this book to life!

And finally, a shout-out to all my taste testers, confidants and friends, who showed me support from the early days and always gave me their honest opinions of when things were overbaked/too salty/too sweet/bland/downright not good. We made it!

Quarto

First published in 2024 by Carnival
an imprint of The Quarto Group.
One Triptych Place, London,
SE1 9SH
United Kingdom
T (0)20 7700 6700
www.Quarto.com

A catalogue record for this book is available
from the British Library.

ISBN 978-0-7112-9252-9
Ebook ISBN 978-0-7112-9253-6

10 9 8 7 6 5 4 3 2 1

Photographer: Maja Smend
Food Stylist: Katy McClelland
Prop Stylist: Lydia McPherson
Designer: Nikki Ellis

Publisher: Eleanor Maxfield
Editorial Director: Nicky Hill
Art Director: Paileen Currie
Senior Production Controller: Rohana Yusof

Printed in China

NOTES

Metric and imperial measurements are given
for all recipes. Use one set only and not a
mixture of both.

All tablespoons and teaspoons are level.

All milk should be full-fat unless otherwise
stated.

All eggs should be UK large eggs or US XL eggs,
unless otherwise stated.